Praise for Reimagining Our Tomorrows

"Rich in detail and powerful in prose, Joe Tankersley absolutely nails it in *Reimaging Our Tomorrows*. At a time of such national angst, this refreshingly optimistic book demonstrates that our future is in our hands. It does not have to suck. By changing our stories, we can change our future. Read this book and discover why. Finish the book and you'll know how. This is a must-read for all doers and dreamers that seek a better tomorrow, starting today."

—Jason Haber, Author *The Business of Good*

"Joe Tankersley wants us to reinvent the world. His stories about the future remind us that we can either be stupefied by the sheer quantity of information we face every day, or we can use imagination—one of human beings' defining characteristics—to transmute all that data, shaping it into visions of a world we want even if we haven't yet experienced it. *Reimagining Our Tomorrows* invites us to influence the course of events, to act as global architects, to exercise agency over the future. As someone who has worked for many years at the nexus of scenario planning, design and complex global challenges, I have come to believe Joe's central message: Our futures depend on imagination."

—Erika Gregory, Managing Director N Square Collaborative: The Crossroads for Nuclear Security Innovation

"This book is a MUST READ for policy makers, civil society leaders, business executives, and religious leaders. Not only does it inspire us, but it takes on the toughest problems we face and shows us how WE can make it a bright future with a sustainable planet! But what makes this book so important is that it gives US ALL HOPE . . . hope for a tomorrow that includes EVERYONE in a just and civil society that protects and nurtures our planet for future generations. Thank you Joe!"

—Richard A. Berman, Associate Vice President Strategic Initiatives and Visiting Professor of Social Entrepreneurship, University of South Florida

"Reimagining our future has never been more exciting; Joe Tankersley takes readers through a future world grounded in reality that is both tantalizing and encouraging. In the nebulous haze that is our collective future, he has written a marvelous, collaborative world for all of us to move forward towards with enthusiasm. As a social entrepreneur, I am recommending this book to every volunteer, supporter, and partner to show what change can bring about, and to open our minds to the possibilities of change."

—Robert Lee, Chief Executive Officer
Rescuing Leftover Cuisine, Inc.

"We are only as powerful as the stories we tell ourselves. With optimism a nd humor, Tankersley's fictional vignettes present a rich view of a not-so-far-off future where individuals use technology to build community, collaborate on positive change and live in harmony with the environment. A quick, inspiring read."

—Tom Szaky, CEO and founder TerraCycle

"Thought-provoking, inspiring, and fun to read! Tankersley visions a future with hope and opportunity."

—Tricia Cerrone, Award-Winning Author

"Reimagining Our Tomorrows is the book we need right now. Using storytelling that's dense with astonishing ideas, futurist Joe Tankersley shows how we create the futures that we imagine. By changing the stories we tell ourselves about what could happen, we can craft the future we want rather than one we fear. *Reimagining Our Tomorrows* is a manual for optimists and a love letter to the transformative power of the human imagination, but it's grounded in reality. Read it and take charge of your future!"

—Karl Schroeder, Futurist and Award-Winning
Science Fiction Author

Reimagining Our Tomorrows

Making Sure
Your Future
Doesn't SUCK

JOE TANKERSLEY

To my daughter Allison

May the futures you create be filled with joy, adventure, and compassion.

First published September 2018

Cover and interior design by Libby Kingsbury

ISBN 978-1-7326281-2-0 (paperback)
ISBN 978-1-7326281-1-3 (ebook)

Published by Unique Visions, Inc.
www.uniquevisions.net
Contact info@uniquevisions.net

Contents

Introduction v

Chapter One: Saying Goodbye to the Past 1
Archibald T. Patterson III Records His Legacy

Chapter Two: Reimagining Aging 12
Al Dreamed of a Viking Funeral

Chapter Three: Reimagining Consumerism 26
Rokeya's Fashionable Statement

Chapter Four: Reimagining Automation 44
Elvis Ivanovich, Robot Lover

Chapter Five: Reimagining the Gig Economy 62
Andy and Sue Plan Their Getaway

Chapter Six: Reimagining Technology Access 76
Fast Sammy, the Two-Wheelin' Grocer

Chapter Seven: Reimagining Suburbia 91
Allie Chase Brings the NEWS!

Chapter Eight: Reimagining Rural Life 108
Vedja Goes on a Date, Sorta

Chapter Nine: Reimagining Sustainability 125
Gabby in Paradise

Chapter Ten: Reimagining Community 140
The Birth of Hope

Conclusion: Cool Stories, Bro! 158
So Now What?

Resources 163

Help Me Spread Optimistic Futures 166

Acknowledgments 167

About the Author 169

Introduction

Do you worry that the future is going to suck? Not just your personal future, but that of your friends, family, even the entire planet? Are you convinced that your tomorrows will be filled with more challenges than opportunities? Well, you're not alone. When the Harvard Institute of Politics interviewed a group of eighteen- to twenty-nine-year-olds, two-thirds said they were fearful about the future.

You have been given plenty of evidence to support your fears. Everywhere you look, from mainstream media to your social media feed, headlines scream about perils just beyond the horizon:

TECHNOLOGY HAS ALREADY STOLEN YOUR PRIVACY

DIGITAL ADDICTION IS DESTROYING YOUR ABILITY TO THINK

AUTOMATION IS GOING TO TAKE YOUR JOB

CLIMATE CHANGE IS THREATENING YOUR VERY EXISTENCE

It's easy to see why you might want to just curl up on your sofa and binge-watch shows from your childhood when life was simpler. Even if you don't believe the future is completely bleak, you probably suffer from a constant feeling that it's getting harder and harder to keep up with what's coming next. It's true; we live in a world where change is happening so fast, it threatens to outpace our imagination.

I want to help you reimagine our tomorrows; to show you that we are living in a time when the possibility of creating a better future has never been greater. Whether you are an entrepreneur, employee of a tiny nonprofit or massive corporation, citizen activist, concerned parent, or student just starting out, you actually have the power to create a future that is sustainable, equitable, and abundant.

This new future begins with the stories we tell ourselves about what's possible. As futurist and author Brian David Johnson observed, "If we want to imagine a better future and then build it we need to change the story we are telling ourselves about the future we want to live in."[1]

In a world where you're constantly being told that preparing for the future means:

GETTING MORE EDUCATION

IMPROVING YOUR SOCIAL MEDIA STANDING

BECOMING MORE TECHNOLOGICALLY LITERATE

---

1 Johnson, Brian David, *Imagining the Future and Building It.* Intel Corp, 2012. 7.

and on and on, I'm going to tell you that changing the future is as simple as changing the stories we tell ourselves? Yep, I am.

For more than three decades, I've been using stories to entertain, educate, and empower. I have seen how stories can motivate anyone to overcome obstacles, create new opportunities, and build realities they hadn't even imagined were possible.

I've always been fascinated by the power of story. Especially stories about the future. Honest confession: I was one of those geeky kids back before it was cool to be a nerd. I spent a large part of my youth hiding in books that transported me to faraway tomorrows. As much as I loved the swashbuckling space operas of writers like Robert Heinlein, I was even more intrigued by Arthur C. Clark, who created worlds I could imagine inhabiting.

Growing up surrounded by those stories, it wasn't surprising that when it came time to start adulting, I became a storyteller. I began my career in television and film and later made my way to Walt Disney Imagineering (WDI), where I helped create stories that entertained millions of people.

Then one day, I discovered how to combine my two passions: storytelling and creating the future. It began with an old video of science fiction writer Ray Bradbury talking about his friend Walt Disney. He described Disney as an *optimistic futurist* because Walt believed that we could create *Great Big Beautiful Tomorrows.* He observed that Walt's primary tool for building those tomorrows were the stories he told about the future. Long before Walt imagined his Experimental Prototype Community of Tomorrow (EPCOT), he used the power of imagination to inspire the future. His very first television series, *Disneyland,* featured regular episodes exploring possible tomorrows.

What Disney did in the last century professional futurists do today using the tools of social science. Futurists work in corporations, government agencies, and educational institutions. Their job is to help organizations shape their futures. They combine research with a deep understanding of how change happens and create stories of possible futures. These stories, just like the ones Walt Disney created, help us imagine the unseen and discover patterns in the unknown.

It didn't take long for me to realize I had been training my entire life to become an optimistic futurist. I convinced my bosses at Imagineering that having their own futurist was as Disney as, well, Mickey Mouse. I helped create and lead a Strategic Foresight Group that was part of WDI's innovation group called the *Blue-Sky Studio.* I imagined and explored possible futures for theme parks, entertainment, media, the workforce, and socially responsible corporations. I helped teach futures-thinking to hundreds of Disney cast members. I combined storytelling with foresight to create a tool for imagining better futures called *Strategic Narratives.*

In 2014, I took those Strategic Narratives on the road and founded Unique Visions to help organizations create better tomorrows. I have worked with major corporations, nonprofits, and community organizations as they reimagine their tomorrows. The results have been overwhelmingly positive. Stories about possible futures expand people's ideas about what is possible and enhance their sense of agency about the future.

This book is intended to share that sense of power and agency to anyone who dreams of creating positive futures. Together, we will create a community of optimistic futurists. Together we will build better tomorrows.

Books about the future typically fall into one of two categories: If they are filled with data about trends and new technology, they tend to be considered nonfiction. If the emphasis is on story, plot, and action, they are called science fiction. Strategic Narratives fall somewhere in between. They are based on trend research and data, wrapped in the elements of story. These speculative hybrids of fact and fiction are tools to provoke conversation and inspire creative strategies.

Each chapter offers a glimpse into a possible tomorrow, set about twenty years in the future. They address some of the most important issues we are grappling with today: technological disruption, economic opportunity, and climate change. These narratives intentionally explore a wide range of communities, individuals, and occupations. The stories share three common elements:

1. They are based on the belief that our best tomorrows will value individual empowerment and support equity.
2. They imagine a future built from the bottom up and outside in, with significant involvement by those who have typically been on the fringes.
3. They demonstrate what is possible when individuals use the tools of our digital age to collaborate and build community.
4. They acknowledge that our future requires us to live in harmony with the planet.

In these tomorrows, individuals trade their jobs for personalized careers built around their passions, disenfranchised neighborhoods are revitalized, seniors enjoy their golden years, and we build communities that respect and restore the natural environment.

These are not utopian dreams. They are all possible, practical tomorrows. But none are inevitable. They will only happen if you choose to create them. Even then, there are forces that will actively oppose our dreams for better tomorrows.

You will be escorted through these futures by a fictional narrator, Archibald T. Patterson. Archie represents those people who have built their power and fortunes on the past. We call them the *1 Percent, the Elites, the Patriarchs of the Old Society.* In our world, most of them are older white dudes. While the details of their backgrounds, ethnicity, and power are specific to the time we live in, their motivations are universal. People like Archie, those privileged by the current system, are not inclined to step aside and go gently into the history books. While I do not expect you to like Archie, you must understand his motives if we are to create a different future. Change is risky and often hard. Even when our actions are clearly doing more long-term harm than good, we often cling to outmoded ideas. Fear is often the most significant barrier to positive change.

If you take only one thing from this book, I hope it is this: **if we change our stories, we can change our tomorrows. You live in a moment when your individual power to shape the future has never been greater.**

It probably comes as no big surprise that while I was working at the Walt Disney Company, I was surrounded by quotes from its founder. One of the most popular of those goes like this: "If you can dream it, you can do it."

Most people tend to focus on the "do it" part. They see it as an affirmation that any idea, no matter how fantastic, can be made into reality. I read the quote differently. I see it as a powerful reminder that nothing is possible if we can't first imagine it.

Our best tomorrows will be born from your dreams.
Be fearless and dream big.

I

Saying Goodbye to the Past

Archibald T. Patterson III Records His Legacy

June 4, 2036

Three thousand four hundred thirty-two books fill the shelves that run floor to ceiling along one wall of Archibald T. Patterson's personal library. The rest of the immense space is an overstuffed museum of curiosities, filled with everything from priceless antiquities to contemporary kitsch. Props from popular sci-fi movies are showcased with the same care and attention as one-of-a-kind historical artifacts. A globe of the moon autographed by nine of the twelve astronauts who walked on it stands next to a carefully arranged collection of models used in the early *Star Wars* movies. The largest known fragment from the Sikhote-Alin meteorite that fell to Earth in 1947 sits on top of an original copy of David Bowie's *Ziggy Stardust* album cover. It would literally take hours to go through the entire collection and even then, it would be difficult to gain much insight into why Archibald Patterson had spent millions of dollars creating this collection. The real answer was because he could.

Sandwiched among the antiquities, tacky souvenirs, and priceless books, three technicians, dressed in white coveralls, carefully unload equipment from half a dozen cases. The cases, 3-D printed using the latest bioplastics, shimmer iridescently, sending sparks of color across the room, adding to the visual cacophony.

The door to the library opens. A hoverchair, carrying Archibald T. Patterson, glides into the room. Archie, as he prefers to be called, is in remarkably good shape for someone about to celebrate his ninetieth birthday. He sits tall in the chair; his shoulders pulled back, head held high. Even confined to the chair, there is no question that he is in charge. He radiates the extraordinary self-confidence that comes from possessing enormous wealth and power.

Archie is followed into the room by his personal secretary, Beverly, and his medibot. The medibot is a white, three-foot-tall cylinder with two retractable arms and a giant round "eye" set on top. Its dumpy exterior hides the fact that it can perform nearly every medical function of a fully equipped hospital emergency room. Having a full-time medical robot is just one of the many technological wonders available to the super rich who use their wealth to slow down, and almost stop, the aging process.

The chair floats across the room, expertly maneuvering among the collection of objects, toward the technicians. They stop what they are doing and await his arrival. The senior tech, a tall, dark-skinned woman in her early thirties, steps forward to greet him. She extends her hand.

"Mr. Patterson, it's truly an honor to meet you, sir. Amelie Hafidi of Lasting Memories. If you have any questions, at all, about your session, I'm happy to answer them for you."

Archie takes her hand. His grasp is firm and friendly. "Well, I'm a curious old fart. Walk me through the process."

"It's really very simple. First, we deploy the cameras." She nods to her team, and eight camera drones pop out of their carrying cases and take up positions around Archie.

"They capture your image in 3-D/360. For reference purposes, we'll be projecting it during the session."

She points toward a massive table in the middle of the room covered haphazardly in what look to be ancient maps. A hologram of Archie's head appears to float gently above them.

"You simply deliver your legacy. If you need to stop and start, no problem—we have complete editing capabilities. After we're done here, we'll translate the digital files into the physical avatar that will live in our memorial garden. Of course, we will also maintain the digital copy for those who might want to access it remotely. Any other questions?"

"Just one. Beverly."

Archie's secretary quickly steps up. She is as precise in her movement as she is in her dress and in her attention to the details of serving her boss. "Yes, sir?"

"Tell me again why I'm doing this?"

Beverly smiles. She has worked for Archie for nearly twenty years now and knows that her boss's cantankerousness is largely an act.

"It's for your grandchildren and their grandchildren, so they will have something to remember you by."

"In perpetuity," Amelie offers helpfully.

Archie scowls, then lets out a long sigh. "Guess I better try and leave them with something useful then."

"Ready to begin whenever you are, Mr. Patterson," Amelie says as she steps back to join the rest of her team.

Archie considers the floating 3-D hologram of himself for a

moment. He turns his head from side to side and the image reacts accordingly. He smiles and the image smiles back. He sticks out his tongue and is greeted with the same. Seemingly satisfied that the hologram won't suddenly revolt and come alive, he sits up even straighter in his chair, clears his throat, and begins:

"My name is Archibald Thaddeus Patterson III. Today is my ninetieth birthday. I have been blessed with a long and privileged life. Later today there will be a grand celebration in honor of the power and wealth that I have accumulated during the course of that life. This party will be attended by many people, most of whom I barely know. They will come because they believe it is still important to see and be seen in the company of those who consider themselves masters of the world. I suspect they are fooling themselves about the importance of their privilege. Nonetheless, I'm sure my staff will make sure they enjoy themselves. At the end of the evening, I will say my goodbyes to my family and the few close friends I have, before retiring to my bedroom, where my medibot will administer the injection that will end my life.

"Members of my family, even the board of directors of my company, have passionately argued against this decision. I am not suffering from any life-threatening conditions. My doctors assure me that my diagnostic forecasts suggest I could easily reach the age of 100. Frankly, I do not see the point. It seems like just another artificial accomplishment and I am quite content with my life's accomplishments.

"On my last day on Earth, what fascinates me are not those accomplishments but rather the events that have taken place in recent years that have transformed the world around me into a place I hardly recognize. You see, I spent most of my adult life believing that I was building the future. Looking back, it seems that I, and many others like me, were busy trying to keep the future from being born.

"Don't get me wrong; we dreamed of great big beautiful tomorrows. Our future was going to be filled with technological marvels that would bring us individual freedoms, success, and, yes, unimaginable wealth. For some of us, the lucky few, those dream became reality. We have become some of the most wealthy and powerful men, and a few women, in all of history. We were the objects of admiration, jealousy, fear, and hatred. We controlled the destiny of nations. We built great corporations that spanned the globe We were the pinnacle of the great industrial age. In our lifetimes we produced more than any generations before us, more of everything; more than we could ever need.

"Too late we began to realize that our great big tomorrows were a Pandora's box of riches. For every advance, there came unexpected and often disastrous side effects. Pesticides promised us abundant harvests but also brought silent springs. A never-ending supply of cheap consumer goods produced tons of garbage that will overflow our landfills for centuries. Our unquenchable thirst for fossil fuels melted the polar ice caps. Of all our sins, I am afraid the worst was that we traded our dreams of building a better future for money and power.

"For much of my life, technology has advanced faster than our imaginations. We simply could not keep up with the powerful forces we had unleashed. So, we retreated into the safety of our power and privilege. At a time when we needed to be looking beyond the horizon for new ideas, new directions, we looked for safety in doing more of the same. We built bigger, faster, cheaper. We decided that our present would become all—all pervasive, all lasting, all we ever needed. But we were wrong.

"I remember there was a writer—Toffler, I believe. I'm sure his book is somewhere on my shelves. He coined a term for what we were feeling. Future Shock he called it. The inability to keep up with 'too much change in too short a period of time.' He called it a disease, and we were its victims.

"Looking back now, it is hard to see how we missed what was really happening. How could we have been so blind not to realize that the great age of technology we created had already given birth to its offspring? An offspring that would grow to become Zeus to our Cronus, destined to steal heaven from us.

"This new world was born of silicon."

Archie pauses and turns to consider Amelie who is focused on his every word.

"You know, young lady, I lived in the time before we had computers. I remember when I saw my first one. It took up the entire floor of a building. It was a massive machine that really wasn't much more than a glorified calculator.

"Oh, but even then, many of us dreamt of what it could become. We imagined machines more powerful than anything we had ever seen. We saw the possibility of using this new technology to make capitalism faster, more efficient, and unlock new sources of wealth and power. It didn't take long for us to begin to realize some of those dreams. But in our zeal, we missed the most important point. These new machines were harbingers of a much more fundamental shift. Maybe if we had heeded the words of Marshall McLuhan, we would have been prepared. He warned us that 'first we built the machines, then they build us.' Maybe. . . . "

Archie coughs. The first one is followed by a second, and a third. Suddenly he is doubled over in a coughing fit. The floating Archie head mimics the convulsions.

The medibot rushes to aid Archie. One of the arms extends and gently rests on the back of his neck. After a brief moment of diagnostics, the hand slides back and is replaced by the nozzle of a needleless jet injector. The nozzle touches Archie's neck and blasts a jet of medicine thinner than a strand of hair under his skin. The drug is fast acting and in less than a minute Archie manages to control his cough.

As the cough dies away, Beverly brings him a glass of water. Archie manages to take a tentative sip, then another, and finally a longer drink. The coughing spell is over. He hands the glass back to Beverly.

Archie looks up; "I must sound like some old geezer, going on and on about the past."

"Your history is fascinating, sir," Amelie quickly responds.

"History is for the dead," Archie replies and swings the hoverchair around toward the wall of books.

"Beverly, come help me. There is a book here somewhere. I don't remember the title. It was by that fellow who once ran the MIT New Media Center. What was his name?"

Beverly blinks a couple of times, activating her internet implant.

"I believe his name was Joi Ito and the book's title," She pauses briefly, looking off into the distance, "was *Whiplash*."

She crosses to the bookcase and goes directly to the book.

"I believe you will find it right here." She pulls out the book and hands it to him.

Archie takes the book and begins to flip through it. He pauses to reread favorite passages.

"Ah yes, there it is."

He floats back across the room and stops in the middle of the hovering cameras. He turns to check on his hologram. The tech has already reactivated it.

"I've spent the better part of the past decade trying to understand how I and so many others missed the promise of this new age.

"It took me a long time and a lot of help," he holds up the book, "to put the pieces together.

"Back in the teens, when I had no inkling that the world I was so invested in was on the brink of disruption, others, like Mr. Ito, were already imagining a radically different future."

He reads a passage from the book:

The Internet and the integrated circuit chip . . . heralded the beginning of the network age, a more distinct break from the industrial era than anything that has occurred before it. . . . When these two revolutions—one in technology, the other in communications—joined together, an explosive force was unleashed that changed the very nature of innovation, relocating it from the center (governments and big companies) to the edges. . . ." [2]

He closes the book and pauses for a moment.

"Of course, those of us who represented the center weren't so keen on turning our power over to those on the fringes. We told ourselves that could only lead to chaos. Honestly, at first, we couldn't imagine how a bunch of garage nerds and smalltime entrepreneurs could challenge us. We were the builders of the world's economies. No one could match our reach and scale.

"When we realized that the economy was fundamentally shifting, we panicked. We banded together to keep this new age to ourselves. We used our networks to manufacture stories of fear and disaster.

---

2 Ito, Joichi, and Jeff Howe. *Whiplash.* New York, NY, Grand Central Publishing, Dec. 2016. 21–25.

We threatened, we cajoled, we pleaded, we bribed. Hell, we bought whole governments and had them pass laws just to protect us from change.

"We almost won. We almost stopped the future from arriving. Fortunately for all of us, we failed.

"We failed because of the dreamers that still lived among us. Some of them were the digital natives who, unencumbered by our analog history, couldn't imagine why we needed to concentrate power in the hands of a few. They were joined by individuals of all ages and backgrounds who had little to lose and everything to gain. They managed somehow to escape the shroud of fear and uncertainty we had so carefully constructed. They were able to see that there was a better tomorrow out there just waiting to be born. They gathered in chat rooms and coffee shops to talk about their dreams. They named their new age The Digital Renaissance.

"Against all our expectations, they began to transform those dreams into realities. This future was born on the fringes."

As Archie continues he becomes more and more excited, leaning forward until he is almost standing up.

"It sprang up in neglected city centers, where young entrepreneurs harnessed technology to feed their neighbors in dying suburbs where new pioneers came determined to restore community and local pride. It was built by aging baby boomers determined to transform old age into the golden years, and by workers of all ages who traded in their jobs for personalized careers built around their passions.

"These dreamers gleefully shared their experiments and invited others to co-create with them. They refused to believe in our economics of scarcity and instead created a world of abundance, sustainability, and equity. They didn't wait for permission but empowered themselves, and in so doing, they empowered everyone."

Archie slumps back down into the chair and takes a long slow breath before continuing quietly.

"It is the curse of all those who are successful to feel the need to leave behind some token of their accomplishments. I am guilty of that pride. So, you can imagine how it feels to realize that the world I worked so hard to build and defend is destined to disappear; replaced by a new and very different one."

Archie pauses. For the first time his self-confidence seems to waver. He has the look of a man uncertain about his past choices.

"My accomplishments, my triumphs soon to be forgotten, and my legacy, reduced to this."

He turns and scowls at the floating holographic head. The head scowls back.

"A narcissist's monument babbling away in a privileged man's graveyard. A ghost talking only to other ghosts."

Archie spins the floating chair around to face the books. The camera drones dart to follow him. He glides along the wall of books, brushing his hand affectionately across the spines. He comes to the end of the room and stops as the drones circle him like flies.

"I have read enough of these books to know that those who create the future often forget the importance of the past."

He guides the chair back toward the middle of the room, a man now lost in nostalgia and rumination. He stops next to the table covered in maps, where his holographic image floats. The two faces stare intently at one another.

"I know you doubt that I have anything to add to your new world, but without us, your future would not have been possible. Oh, I know that I have admitted we did everything we could to stop it, but maybe we were simply playing our role. You must remember, the oyster does not make a pearl unless there is a grain of sand that first serves as an irritant. By holding on too tightly to the past we were the grain of sand that sparked the disruptions needed to launch this next age of human accomplishment.

"At the very least, as you continue to build this new world where technology and social progress have unleashed individual empowerment, I will be the voice explaining what it took to get you here. You may think my words are little more than a transparent effort at self-justification. So be it. But I do hope you will learn at least one lesson from my observations. The power to create the future comes with great responsibility. You must use it wisely."

2

Reimagining Aging

Al Dreamed of a Viking Funeral

The Viking longboat floated gently on the black water in the middle of the small lake. The night stars glistened off the bronze shields that lined the boat's side. In the center of the boat was a pyre, built of rough-hewn timber and filled with dry straw and strong meadow herbs that would give the fire its fragrance as it burned. Every detail of the scene seemed perfectly authentic. Well, every detail except for Al, dressed in his favorite Smokey Mountain Herschend Family Park T-shirt, faded jeans, and bright orange Keds, stretched out on top of the pyre.

The kindling burst into flames with a giant roar that made Jack lean away. He could feel the heat from the flames on his face. The air filled with the scent of the herbs—it was a strong, musky, earthy fragrance that made Jack think of hot days, sweating in the summer sun. In the distance, a mournful bagpipe played "Will the Circle be Unbroken," as Al's body returned to the great beyond.

The last notes of the song faded away, and the fire began to smolder. Jack sensed that Celeste had let go of his left hand. Likewise, he released his grip on Charlie's hand to his right. He said goodbye one last time to his old friend and removed his VR headset.

The world swirled in and out of focus. Jack struggled to keep his balance. He closed his eyes and forced himself to take a long, slow, deep breath. He could feel his equilibrium returning, and he opened his eyes.

This time the world around him came into clear focus, and he could see the seven others who had been standing in a circle, holding hands, all dealing with the same jarring shift caused by stepping out of the virtual and back into the real. None of them had grown up with VR, and so they all felt the effects much more than younger generations that moved easily between worlds.

Jack considered what it meant to be a member of the last generation able to make a distinction between real and virtual life. He didn't care much for the entertainment VRs that dominated the popular culture. He did appreciate the virtual pain management apps on those days when his arthritis was acting up, which was happening more and more frequently these days.

VPM's were way more effective than anything the pharmas offered, at a fraction of the cost and with much fewer serious side effects. Jack thought it was such a strange irony that the big drug companies could still find a market for their twentieth-century patent medicines when there were so many virtual and holistic treatments for almost every ailment and many serious diseases.

Like most ironies, this one had as much to do with perceived status as reality. Even today, the wealthiest members of his generation, who could afford any treatment, selected some of the most ineffective, simply because they were expensive. If it weren't for blind acceptance by this one segment of the aging population, big pharma would have already disappeared, just like private insurance did a decade ago. Soon enough, they would vanish along with much of the "real" world that so many of their users clung to so tightly.

Of course, many of those same uber-wealthy, older individuals were also the most avid consumers of the newest VRs. The latest trend was in bespoke entertainments—fantasies designed to meet an individual's every dream and desire, even the ones they might not be willing to admit to their closest friends or family. Jack preferred watching the real birds that gathered around the feeders in the courtyard or debating religion, politics, or the meaning of reality with his good friend Al.

Since they had first met in middle school, long before the *Matrix* movies, Al had spent countless hours trying to convince him that they were all part of a giant computer simulation. It had been the topic of their last conversation just three days before he died. Jack had no idea if his friend was right, or even serious about the idea. Whatever this world was, he was sure it was going to be much emptier without Al.

"I'm going to miss you dude," he whispered. Jack turned and walked across the patio to the sliding bamboo doors that separated his and Celeste's unit from the home's courtyard. The others had already disappeared inside their units. Later, they would come back together around the large wooden table in the middle of that same courtyard to celebrate Al. They would share stories about their friend and housemate and ruminate on the ways their own lives were winding down. There would be food, wine, and even a little misuse of medical cannabis. It was a tradition that was becoming more and more familiar.

It wasn't that death came as a surprise to them. They had all moved into the senior co-op in their late seventies, intending to share their final years together. The original group had included Jack and Celeste, Al and Sharon, Danny and Bridgette, Mark and Patty.

They had been friends for decades. They planned, discussed, and debated all the details of their plan to remain independent. The co-op's layout was simple: four units surrounding a common courtyard. They had built the home on an oversized residential lot in the middle of town, after winning a protracted fight with the city over outdated zoning regulations. The property was large enough for an art studio, spacious garden, and separate apartment unit for their caregivers.

All eight were in seemingly good health when they first moved in, so they had been able to avoid the more difficult conversations about end-of-life decisions. Three years later, when Sharon died unexpectedly, they realized they had not planned for the obvious outcome of their decision. The heated and emotional arguments over what kind of service Sharon would have wanted was a surprise and in some ways the first real challenge to the idyllic *golden years* they had crafted for themselves.

Celeste, always the practical one, suggested that they come up with some rules about how they would celebrate and grieve together. They all agreed that each person would write down specific instructions for their send-off. For future residents, this would be a requirement before they could move into the co-op. As long as the deceased or their partner could cover the costs, there would be no limits put on the requests. Al had argued that memorial services were really for those left behind. He proposed that the service be followed by a dinner, with the menu chosen by the deceased—as a final gift to the others.

A seriousness settled over the co-op for the next few weeks as everyone set about the task of defining their departure. What surprised them the most was that once they finished, they all felt as if a giant burden had been lifted. Life soon returned to normal.

For the next five years, everyone remained healthy, and the trauma of facing death was largely forgotten, at least in everyday conversations. Instead, they focused on building a new type of family. Living together in the co-op provided them with the mix of independence and community they needed.

They actively watched after one another, a task that helped to keep them alert and healthy. Jack and Al built raised beds in the garden for Bridgette to accommodate her wheelchair. Mark had been the co-op's tech guy, helping the others learn how to use the various new devices designed to make life easier. Lately, they had all taken to checking in when they woke in the morning, just in case.

Of course, they couldn't do everything for themselves. For those tasks, there was technology and, most importantly, Carl and Celia, their caregivers. The young couple, and their now twelve-year-old daughter, Eventine, had lived with them for nearly eight years now. Carl was a trained geriatric nurse. His primary responsibility was diagnosing the constant stream of personal medical data that everyone's wearable devices collected. He also had to listen to daily complaints about new aches and pains and make sure the more serious ones were looked after.

Celia was an amazing chef. She had been a barista and poet before coming here with Carl. She quickly learned the secrets of cooking tasty and nutritious geriatric meals, and they had eaten like royalty ever since. Celia also did the heavy work in the garden.

Eventine was the most important part of the team. She refused to let any of her *grand-people* consider themselves old. She had an instinct for showing up whenever one of them was feeling down. She would innocently ask for help with some project, giving them an excuse to focus on someone other than themselves.

Even her youthful exuberance couldn't keep away the inevitable. Mark was the next to go—the victim of a long-dormant genetic inheritance that caused his heart to fail. His wife, Patty, died just a couple of months later, seemingly of a broken heart. The couple had been together for more than seventy years.

Amy and Saro had barely gotten settled into the empty unit when Danny and Bridgette announced to the house that they had decided it was their time. The decision didn't come as a complete surprise. All had agreed that they would respect each other's end of life decisions. Still, it threatened to upset the emotional balance of the home. Recognizing this, the couple planned an elaborate and moving celebration for their final day.

Less than a year later, Saro died. Her partner Amy took the loss hard and for weeks refused to come out of her apartment. Al started sleeping on her couch to make sure that she wasn't alone. After a while, he moved his stuff into her unit, and the house looked for a new couple to fill the second empty unit. Charlie and Lloyd were the first youngsters (both in their early seventies) to join the group. Their arrival provided a needed infusion of energy and hope.

Now they had lost Al. His request for "a full Viking funeral" had been by far the most flamboyant, but given his character, it hadn't come as a surprise to any of his housemates. Certainly, not to Jack, his closest friend. Al had made sure his request wasn't a burden by commissioning his granddaughter, an accomplished VR designer, to create the simulation. The day before the memorial, Jack accompanied his friend's body to the local crematorium. In a few days, he would retrieve the ashes and ship them to Al's daughter in Florida.

She would be responsible for spreading them at sea—an action that was of dubious legality but a fitting final resting place for someone who had so loved the water.

In acknowledgment of their failing stamina, it had become their habit to each go back to their own spaces for a while before these memorial meals. They would take their afternoon nap, read or meditate, or take the time to catch up with their families spread across the globe.

Jack and Celeste went to their bedroom without a word. They lay down on the top of the bed and rolled toward each other. They hugged for a very long time.

Finally, Celeste gave him a quick peck on the forehead, rolled away and said, "Old age isn't for sissies."

Jack smiled a big broad smile and replied, "Life is wonderful, my dear."

With that, he closed his eyes. He felt her get up and leave the room. He slept soundly for just over forty-five minutes before Rosie, their smart agent, gently alerted him that he was in the optimum biorhythm state to end his nap.

He padded out to the kitchen/living room expecting to find Celeste puttering around like she often did when she was upset. Instead, he discovered that the only puttering going on was the Roomba, wandering in a seemingly aimless pattern around the kitchen floor. Jack sometimes swore that the device sprang into action only when it sensed one of them was about to enter the room. When he had explained his theory about the robot's paranoia, Celeste had given him that look and wondered aloud how she had ended up with a crazy old man. He knew he was robopomorphizing, but given how much it, and their other technologies, seemed to anticipate their needs, it was hard to imagine that they were just well-designed software.

"Rosie, where is Celeste?"

The home control system responded, "She is in the studio. Should I let her know you are looking for her?"

"No thanks."

The studio was Celeste's real refuge. A sculptor all her life, she could not imagine living without making art. She was rarely alone. All the occupants considered art as therapy of one sort or another, even if they didn't consider themselves artists. Denny had proven himself the exception.

Shortly after they moved in, he decided to take up wood carving, something Danny hadn't done since his dad had taught him to whittle, back when Danny was a kid. It didn't take him long to get better than good. Of course, that was another advantage of VR and mixed reality. You could learn almost any skill if you had time and focus. It turned out Danny had both, and before long, he was selling his work to clients around the world.

Jack thought about going out and joining Celeste. The cool clay would feel good against his gnarled fingers. Then he noticed the box of books in the middle of the floor. They had been Al's, just a tiny fraction of the man's library. They had all ribbed him about his obsession with collecting old-fashioned books. Sharon had joked that after she was gone, he'd probably fill her side of the bed up with books. Amy, who had been a fantasy writer when she was younger, was convinced that Al had tapped into an alternate universe and was squirreling books away in a vast secret library. One of the nice things about growing old with creative people was that their craziness tended to be more imaginative than most.

In the final weeks before his death, Al had gotten rid of all the books but these few that, for one reason or another, held special meaning for him. He had assigned Jack the task of deciding how to distribute them. Jack sat down on the floor and pulled the first book from the box. He read the spine and thought it might be worth reading. For now, Jack decided that the best course would be to put them on the bookshelf before Celeste returned. She liked to keep their nest neat and tidy. Jack appreciated that, even though he was a natural slob. He was most comfortable when surrounded by chaos; something about the mess energized him. He suspected it was his ADD, a condition he had struggled against most of his life. It was only in the last few years that he had relaxed and accepted it as part of who he truly was.

At some point, you just quit worrying about not being the perfect version of yourself. It also helped that neuroscience had made significant leaps forward and it was finally possible to understand how the brain worked. That understanding brought with it the realization that all the time spent trying to identify, label, and then erase the personality traits that made us individuals was not only a waste of time but counterproductive.

Jack, long an avid follower of science, was fascinated by the new research coming out of the most advanced neurobiology institutes in India, focusing on celebrating these differences and helping individuals learn how to apply them in the best possible way. For Jack and the others, the main benefit of these advances came in the form of treatments to ward off the most common mental ailments of old age.

Alzheimer's had nearly disappeared. Dementia was only a problem with the very frail or very old, mainly those over one hundred years old. They had not erased aging, and death still came to everyone, but they had eliminated the fear of having to face decades of deteriorating mental capacity.

Celeste was still right, getting old wasn't for sissies. Some days were worse than others. Jack seemed to lose his reading glasses at least once a day. Every time he did, Celeste would remind him that he could just have the corrective surgery and throw the glasses away.

"I'm too damned old to be a cyborg," Jack would always respond. "If you want a six-billion-dollar man you need to go get yourself one of them sixty-five-year-old kids."

They would laugh and search the unit, sometimes every room—the kitchen, living room, master bedroom, even the second bedroom they used as a study—before finding them in the most obvious place. More often than not, they would be buried under a pile of hand-drawn sketches of birds Jack had been working on and forgotten. They didn't mind these scavenger hunts. It gave them a chance to be active and to laugh at themselves. Along with companionship, these were the most important medicines for growing old successfully.

Jack had one last book to put away when Rosie interrupted, "Celia wants you to know that dinner is almost ready."

He slid the last book onto the shelf. He realized he had been sitting on the floor for some time, and it was unlikely he could get up by himself. He was only mildly surprised to see that the Roomba had already sidled up to his side, just within arm's length. He scooted himself on top of the robot. Once he was in place, it slowly rose from the floor to its full height, carrying Jack upright. When he was standing, he turned and looked down at the robot.

"Don't be looking so smug. Remember I was sitting on your face." He couldn't resist the impulse to give it an affectionate pat. Mission accomplished, the robot collapsed back down onto the floor and wandered off.

He could hear the others already gathering in the courtyard. As he headed toward the door, he wondered what dish Al had picked for him. Something sardonic most likely—Al had a wicked sense of humor. Whatever it was, he looked forward to savoring every bite, just as he looked forward to savoring every moment of these years spent together with friends who had become his final family.

Archie's Apology

What were we supposed to do when 10,000 boomers started turning sixty-five every day? They called it the silver tsunami. Some of us referred to it as the *gerontocalpyse*.

How the heck were we going to provide thirty years of services to 75 million baby boomers with a system built for their grandparents, most of whom died before reaching sixty-five?

We had promised them their golden years. The best we had to offer were overcrowded nursing homes staffed with underpaid workers. Even that was a short-term profit play. Who was going to pay for even the most basic accommodations when the government payouts dried up? We had been robbing their pension funds and social security for decades.

They were just supposed to go away and disappear. But it quickly became obvious that this generation wasn't going to go quietly into that dark night. While we worried about ways to prop up a crumbling system, they got busy and started building a new version of old age for themselves.

Imagine our surprise, when baby boomers stepped forward to own the wisdom, challenges, and opportunities that came with growing older. Instead of retreating to the gated communities that were designed to keep anyone under the age of fifty-five out, they demanded to stay in the middle of the action. They refused, or couldn't afford, to quit working. They moved downtown to be close to the restaurants and bars that were supposed to be for partying millennials. These new elders had no interest in being apart from the rest of the community.

The generation that had grown up in their cars began to regard personal automobiles as a hassle and inconvenience. In large cities and small towns, citizen groups demanded communities provide access for everyone. Walkable neighborhoods, mass transit, and innovative ride-sharing systems replaced automobiles as the preferred forms of transportation. By the middle of the 2020s, cars were starting to disappear from downtown districts. Seniors walked more, which made them healthier and able to be even more engaged in the community.

The movement to reintegrate living, working, and commercial spaces exploded in urban areas and the suburbs. During the teens and early twenties, new micro-city centers began to pop up in sleepy bedroom communities. These changes befitted people of all ages, not just seniors. It sparked the biggest boom in locally owned businesses that we had seen in decades.

They were the first generation of digital elders. They might not have grown up in a digital world, but they had been using computers for decades, and they weren't going to stop just because they hit some arbitrary age. As they mixed more with younger generations, they became even more comfortable with the latest technologies.

Smart homes were a boon to elders, making it possible to extend independent living by as long as a decade or more. Wearable computers and telemedicine made it possible to deal with the inevitable challenges of aging bodies without becoming captive to an entrenched, and failing, healthcare system. Dramatic advances in robotics helped to avert the looming shortage of caregivers and senior companions.

All these changes opened the door to rethinking senior housing. More elders abandoned segregated senior developments for new co-housing arrangements, co-ops, and homes intentionally designed to accommodate multiple generations. Corporations that had built their fortune by warehousing seniors in assisted living facilities and nursing homes saw their customer base dwindle.

It was like the baby boomers decided that their one last legacy would be to transform our cultural ideas about growing old. The younger generations were more than happy to join them in imagining a new silver lining to old age.

3

Reimagining Consumerism

Rokeya's Fashionable Statement

The greyish green goop dripping from the nozzle of the 3-D printer was not what Rokeya needed to see. The printer was supposed to be giving birth to a brightly colored, gently flowing sundress, not something that resembled elephant diarrhea. As she watched the material plop and ooze onto the printer's catch tray, it seemed like the perfect image for what was turning out to be a really shitty day. She tried to fight back the tears but couldn't and found herself crying, again.

Rokeya did not look like the kind of woman easily moved to tears. She was in her late thirties, thin, and muscular. She wore a tight-fitting T-shirt with a faded image of a Bengal tiger on the front. Her curve-hugging jeans were so old that the areas covered by colorful patches far exceeded the original denim. Her arms, from elbow to wrist, were covered in brightly colored Bangla script and geometric designs. Her black hair was cut in a short bob, which had the unexpected effect of softening her more masculine features.

Rokeya surrendered herself to the flood of emotions and let the tears flow. Her mother had taught her long ago that a good cry was sometimes needed. It didn't take long for the release to run its course. She wiped away the last of the tears with the back of her hand and pulled herself up tall. She wondered why the morning's incident had affected her so.

She had been returning from a meeting with a group of peer-to-peer investors when it happened. She was already feeling vulnerable. Despite her best efforts, the group hadn't been particularly interested in providing the funding she needed to expand Fatafati Fashion Co-op.

The man who had verbally assaulted her had sagging, yellowed skin. He was sitting on the sidewalk with a crudely lettered sign soliciting handouts. Rokeya had noticed with irony that despite his tattered clothes he had a brand-new chip scanner to accept donations. Even from a distance, she could tell that he hadn't bathed for some time. Still, she had veered toward him, intending to pass him a few creds, as she usually did. As she got close, he looked up and saw her. Their eyes made contact, and his grew dark. He spat out the words with a ferociousness that caused her to stumble.

"What the fuck are you looking at, raghead?! Quit stealing our benefits, get a job! Go back to the shithole you came from!" Spit flew from his lips as he screamed.

Others on the crowded sidewalk paused and looked, first at the man and then at the target of his scorn. Rokeya was too startled to respond. She ducked her head and hurried past him. His taunts followed her all the way to the end of the block.

Once she had finally put enough distance between herself and the angry man to extinguish his voice, she forced herself to slow her pace. She took a deep breath and tried to understand what had just happened. Oh, it wasn't the first time in her life that she had been the target of some racist slur. Growing up a child of poor Bangladeshi immigrants in a town that was predominantly white, she had often been made to feel the other. But that had been years ago before shifting demographics had transformed the city streets into a cosmopolitan jumble of global cultures. There was nothing particularly unusual about a dark-skinned woman walking on the street this morning. Why had he picked her out of the crowd, she wondered?

She caught her reflection in a shop window. Her skin was darker than most and her jet-black hair and eyes the color of coal betrayed her heritage. On the other hand, she was impeccably dressed and professional looking. Rokeya, of all people, appreciated the importance of clothing. She had carefully chosen her outfit for the business meeting that morning. It was one of her original designs: a brightly colored kameez over a pair of dark hemp pants. The long shirt had been upcycled from her mother's closet. In its former life, it had been a brightly colored sari her mother kept for formal occasions. The hemp pants were one of the few pieces in Rokeya's wardrobe made from virgin fabric. They were expensive but well worth the cost; durable and incredibly comfortable. She expected to wear them for many years to come.

As she contemplated her reflection, she recognized the part of her outfit that had probably triggered him. The hijab was handcrafted from the finest jamdani fabric. Tiny white flowers and beige geometric shapes covered the distinctive cobalt-blue background. The headscarf had belonged to Rokeya's grandmother. Rokeya wore it purely as a fashion statement. She, like most of her contemporaries, was Muslim in name only. To her, wearing the hijab was no different than a man wearing his favorite hat.

A sound like a loud burp pulled Rokeya back to the present. The 3-D printer had puked out the last of the goopy mess. She carefully scraped it up and dropped it into a bucket. The material landed with a slurpy thud and jiggled like gruesome Jell-O before collapsing onto itself. She hoisted the bucket and headed to the lab to show Buddy the results of their latest effort to finally make 3-D–printed clothing a practical reality.

Buddy's lab was on the other side of the cavernous facility that had originally been built as a plastics recycling center. Rokeya's Fatafati Fashions Co-op was just one of two dozen craft designers and makers who now shared the space with the recycling operation. The others produced everything from clothes to household items and even specialized industrial equipment. All had chosen the location to be close to a nearly unlimited supply of raw materials in the form of recycled plastic.

When Rokeya and her partners had decided to co-locate here, it had seemed like the perfect plan. At the time, everyone was talking about how clothes made from recycled plastics were the future of sustainable fashion. The technology had advanced rapidly during the teens, and the quality of the materials was superior to traditional fabrics like cotton. It was even becoming possible to print finished garments from plastics that didn't look like costumes from a low budget sci-fi VR. Rokeya, like so many others, was convinced that the world had discovered a sustainable solution to meet the insatiable demand for fast fashion.

Unfortunately, that dream was short-lived. It turned out that every time the clothes were washed, they shed millions of plastic microfibers. The damage caused by these microscopic pollutants was exponentially worse than anything seen before. Some of the mass manufacturers tried to push forward with the plan. They developed elaborate and expensive schemes to capture the pollutants and even eliminate the need for regular washing.

For Rokeya, those were not options. She had started the co-op to serve her two passions; making beautiful clothes and protecting the environment. So, she and her partners shifted to a range of other tactics, including remending, upcycling waste clothes, and recycling natural fabrics. They never gave up on the idea of perfecting 3-D printing. Their holy grail remained to produce a biofiber ink that would let them go directly from design to finished garment without harming the environment. Discovering that ink had become Buddy's obsession.

So, Rokeya was not surprised to find Buddy absorbed in his work when she finally made it to the lab. His tall frame was hunched awkwardly over a piece of brightly colored fabric stretched on a rack. He was wearing his favorite frayed lab coat that looked like it had been used as a canvas for a kindergarten finger-painting class, as he poked and prodded at the fabric.

Rokeya had to weave her way through a maze of vats growing kelp, fabric extruders that turned seaweed into fiber, and tables covered with a wild assortment of scientific-looking equipment. Buddy truly was a mad scientist. He could produce fiber from almost any form of biowaste. Wood pulp, grape skins, mushrooms, orange peels. You name it, and Buddy had probably made it into a material that could be spun, dyed, cut, sewn, and worn. Lately, he had been working with his own strain of lab-grown kelp that he was certain he could transform into a practical fiber ink.

Rokeya stopped a few feet away from Buddy and dropped the bucket to the floor. The thud of plastic on concrete jarred him from his work. He noticed her for the first time and stepped closer to see what she had deposited on his floor.

"What's this?" he asked.

"It's supposed to be my dress printed from your kelp," she answered.

"Damn," he replied, as he bent over the bucket and tipped it to the side to swirl the ugly liquid around. "Damn. I thought I had it this time."

He reached over to the nearest table covered in instruments and rummaged around until he found the one he was looking for. He picked up a long cylindrical device and stuck it into the substance in the bucket. He leaned in closer to read the display. After a moment he stood up and turned to Rokeya. She sensed he was about to go into one of his long-winded explanations about how the molecular structure of the fiber had failed. As much as she enjoyed these arcane scientific conversations, she just didn't have the time or the focus today. She patted him on the shoulder reassuringly.

"Hey, I'm sure you'll sort it out. It's not like anybody thought that coming up with the perfect material for a completely closed loop, zero-waste clothing system, was going to be easy."

She turned and headed toward the door. As she left, she called back over her shoulder. "Just let me know when you're ready to try another batch. In the meantime, I have a 3-D printer to clean up."

Buddy watched her leave and then hauled the bucket from the floor to a spot on the work table with a sigh.

Rokeya had barely gotten out of the lab when the alarm on her wrist chirped brightly. She checked the reminder and saw that she was supposed to be meeting a client for a final fitting in just ten minutes. With all the stress of the morning, she had completely forgotten. Bill Withers was one of her regular clients. He was coming in to pick up his bespoke wedding suit.

Elliott, her lead sewist, was working on finishing the suit and she had intended to check on him when she got back from her morning meeting. The cutting room was all the way on the other side of the facility, close to the print shop. As she turned around and headed back in that direction, she hoped that Elliott had handled everything.

To get to the cutting room, Rokeya had to pass by the remending workshop. The workshop was a maker's space for clothing. For a small fee, anyone could join. The co-op offered classes, access to professional equipment, and one of the largest dead stock collections in town. Most people used the workshop to mend favorite items or add a simple embellishment or two to transform an old garment into something new.

The co-op made sure that there were always a few volunteers around to help out. These were usually teenagers who had started hanging out at the workshop and over time, became part of the family. The most dedicated would start out mending a few things and progress to creating original pieces. Some of the volunteers went on to become shop apprentices. Elliott had started out like that before he graduated to become a full co-op member.

Rokeya knew she didn't have time to stop in but slowed just to take a peek inside the workshop as she passed. Across the room, Tanya, a bubbly middle-aged mother of Iranian-Ugandan descent was overseeing a table of young teens. When she saw Rokeya at the door, she stopped what she was doing and ran toward her. Tanya grabbed Rokeya by the arm and pulled her into the workshop.

"Roke, come see. Look what my little seamstresses are making." As she dragged Rokeya across the room, the words flew out. "They've all been remending their school uniforms. They desperately needed it; they were all so ancient. When their teacher first brought them in she was going to have them just patch and sew. But that would have been so boring. I convinced her to make it a learning module. I told her they could even get credit toward a fashion cert if they needed and now they are making the most beautiful things. Come, come! You have to see."

Tanya and Rokeya stopped in front of the table where the amateur designers were working. Their various projects were piled on top of one another in a way that made Rokeya think of a crazy quilt.

"Children, show Missy Roke your work."

Some of the kids were shy at first, but slowly they managed to untangle the mess, and each held up their outfit for the designer to see. What had been plain grey shorts and white button-down shirts were transformed into a rainbow of colors. Some of the patches were carefully placed to cover tears or holes, but the teens had let their imaginations run wild and transformed their generic uniforms into personal statements. Rokeya stepped closer and looked at them with serious appraisal. She reached out to tug at a patch here and there to make sure they were securely attached.

As she stepped back, she commented; "Wow this is very good. I wish I'd had such beautiful school uniforms when I was your age. I might have made better grades even."

She laughed, and the children joined in. Rokeya hugged Tanya. "Excellent work. Keep it up."

As she started to leave, Tanya called out after her; "Roke, don't forget we're doing a coat drop for the free market this afternoon."

Rokeya smiled and continued toward the cutting room. For the first time, her day seemed to be getting brighter. She loved to design clothes for other people but to be honest, she often thought that the remending workshop was probably the best thing they did at the co-op. The reuse movement had grown so much that it was making a real impact on the number of clothes that were thrown away every year. And the joy that people got when they realized they could unleash their creativity and transform generic, mass-produced junk into pieces that were so personal was unmatched. Of course, Rokeya recognized the irony of the situation. As she and her fellow designers championed the slow fashion movement by promoting remending, recycling, and no waste, they were creating fewer opportunities for themselves to create new clothes. She often wondered if they would ever be so successful that they weren't needed anymore. She doubted it, but at the same time, realized it wouldn't be such a terrible outcome. She could always go back to being a sewist. Until that day, there would still be plenty of demand for special-occasion jobs like the bespoke wedding suit she needed to be checking on.

When Rokeya finally made it to the cutting room, she saw that Bill had already arrived. He and Elliott were watching the robotic seaming machines assemble Bill's suit. Bill was a big hulk of a Midwestern man, tanned from a lifetime of working outdoors. Elliott was opposite in almost every way, pale, slender, androgynous. Rokeya smiled at the odd pairing and tapped Bill on the shoulder. He turned toward her and gave her a great big bear hug.

"Sorry I'm late," Rokeya said as she let herself be consumed by his embrace.

Bill released her and waved off the apology with a hand toughened by years of manual labor.

"No problem. I could watch these things work all day. They move so dang fast." He gestured toward the robot arms clustered around the pieces of his suit that were being hung and assembled on a mannequin. The mannequin had been printed from a 3-D scan of Bill's body to match his measurements. It was so accurate that the left leg was exactly two centimeters shorter than the right, a fact that Bill himself had never known.

Elliott turned to join the conversation. "Just about done. Couple minutes more."

"Everything looking good?" she asked.

"Perfect. Right to spec. It should fit like a glove."

Bill patted his firm stomach. "Hope you included some room to grow. You know what they say about married men getting fat and happy." He laughed.

"No problem Bill. Anytime it needs changes, bring it in. We'll make sure it lasts a lifetime, no matter how happy you get," Rokeya replied, and they all laughed.

"I'm not worried; you've always taken good care of me," Bill said with a smile.

Being the subject of the conversation made Rokeya feel uneasy, so she stepped closer to the cutting floor and turned her attention to the robots as they put the final touches on the suit. Inwardly the praise meant a lot to her, and she knew it was deserved. Bill had been one of her first customers when she had started mending clothes.

He was one of the many construction workers that had been part of the Smart Infrastructure Project of 2025. They had worked to modernize and digitally enhance roads, bridges, tunnels, and public spaces all across the country. It had been hard physical labor, and many of the local workers had started coming to Rokeya's little kiosk to have their work clothes patched and mended. Her business started to take off when she began making original work clothes from a hemp fabric that was tougher and way more comfortable than the cheap mass-market stuff that most of them were wearing. That's how she had met Buddy. The hemp fabric was one of his special blends.

Before long, she had a steady clientele of guys and gals like Bill who would only trust her to make and maintain their work clothes.

Long after the project ended, many of them remained loyal customers. They came to her for special occasions or sometimes just to redesign a favorite piece. She became close friends with many of them. They could have bought their clothes from one of the remaining big labels for less money, but she had shown them that the investment in quality clothing paid for itself over time.

Of course, not everyone was willing to limit their wardrobe to just a few choices. That's why Fatafati Fashions also offered a clothing subscription service. Members paid a monthly fee for access to just about anything in the co-op's wardrobe, even the very expensive special occasion pieces. Rokeya had a few customers who made sure they never wore the same outfit twice.

The robots finished their work and retreated to their stations. Elliott walked over to the mannequin and carefully removed the suit. He escorted Bill to the changing area.

When Bill stepped out a few minutes later wearing the new suit, even Rokeya was impressed by how well it fit. The design was one of her originals. It was a classically cut suit rendered in a contemporary fabric that reimagined traditional Bengali patterns. The suit had been made from refibered material that reflected light in a way that made it almost iridescent. That was another one of Buddy's inventions. The effect was an understated futurism, different but familiar.

"How does it feel?" Rokeya asked.

"Perfect," Bill replied as he flexed his broad shoulders and the suit effortlessly flexed with him. He opened the coat and admired the lining. He ran his hand over the soft material.

"Wow, this feels like silk."

Rokeya smiled. "Actually, it was denim, once upon a time, before Buddy got hold of it."

Bill noticed the label stitched over the inside pocket. The Fatafati logo and name were embroidered in bright blue. Underneath were the words:

Jatra shubhô hok

Bill looked at Rokeya quizzically. "What?"

"Our motto, based on a traditional Bengali saying. It translates more or less to mean *good luck in the journey.*"

"Looking like this, I can't imagine having anything else. Hey, you guys are all coming to the wedding, right? Everybody in the neighborhood is going to be there."

Elliot responded first. "Like duh, miss a party? No way, man."

Later that afternoon, Rokeya was deep in the flow, sketching a new design, when Tanya came bursting into her office.

"Roke, it is time. We will be late for the free market if we do not go now."

Rokeya reluctantly laid down her smartpen. She got up and put on what looked like a classic leather jacket. It was actually 100 percent vegan, made from mycelium grown in Buddy's lab. As she was following Tanya toward the door, she noticed the hijab tossed on her work table. She hesitated and then grabbed it, wrapping it expertly around her head as she walked. *I will not be bullied*, she thought to herself.

At the civic center where the free market took place every month, Rokeya and Tanya quickly unloaded the coats and displayed them on the table set up for them. It was just one of many, covered with everything from toiletries to fully cooked meals, that filled the main auditorium. A long line of men, women, and children waited patiently for the free market to begin.

They had distributed about half of their inventory when Rokeya saw him. It was the old man from the street. He recognized her at the same moment. For a second time in one day, their eyes locked. Then suddenly he looked away. Rokeya watched as he shuffled along in the line, getting closer and closer, never once looking in her direction. When he finally arrived at Rokeya's table, he kept his eyes down and extended his hand toward the pile of coats. Rokeya selected one that looked like it might fit his body.

"You should try it on, make sure it fits. If not, we have others," She fought to control the resentment that she could feel welling up inside as she handed him the coat.

He mumbled, "It'll be fine."

The old man took the coat and shuffled off. After a few steps, he paused and turned, looking straight at her. She could see every bloodshot vein in his puffy eyes.

"Thank you," he said softly, as he clutched the coat tightly.

Rokeya watched as he turned and disappeared into the crowd. She could feel the tears starting to well up in her eyes. She forced herself to take a deep centering breath and wiped the moistness away. As she went back to handing out coats she was barely aware of the smile that had broken free across her face.

Archie's Apology

I am not going to apologize for the consumer economy. It was one of the single greatest accomplishments of modern capitalism. The production and manic marketing of cheap consumer goods created jobs, moved people into the middle class, and made it possible for the average person to own more than the wealthiest kings of history. I have to admit, I never completely got the allure. For as long as I can remember, all of my suits were hand-tailored.

I did understand the economics. The system ran on constant consumption. As long as people kept buying, the economy kept spinning. It turned out that fashion was prime for this model. In one century, we went from a society where the average person had less than ten outfits in their closet to one where they were buying at least that many new outfits every month—outfits that they might wear one or two times before replacing them with next week's must-have look. We called this perpetual buying machine fast fashion.

The key was keeping everything cheap. Cheap resources, cheap labor, cheap energy for transportation. As long as we had all those elements, we could deliver cheap clothing to the consumers and they would buy, buy, buy.

Sure, there were hidden costs. Take cotton for example. Even in the age of man-made materials, cotton remained the king of fashion. Sixty to seventy percent of clothes had at least some cotton in them. For all its image as *the natural choice*, cotton was an environmental nightmare. It took 700 gallons of water to make a single T-shirt, most of which ended up getting dumped into streams and rivers where it killed fish and destroyed habitats. Then, there was the energy required. By the time you added up what it took to grow, harvest, manufacture, and transport those T-shirts, it shouldn't have come as a surprise that the fashion industry was the second largest polluter in the world.

Fortunately for us, all of that was happening far away from the brightly lit malls where the customers were mobbing the racks. The young fashionistas were too busy posting selfies to be concerned about the trail of destruction being left in their wake. We certainly weren't going to bring it up.

The first crack in our perfect plan came on April 24, 2013, when an overcrowded garment factory in Bangladesh collapsed, killing over 1000 workers. The international coverage of the incident shined a bright light on the exploitation at the heart of the industry. The marketplace demanded that something be done, and we responded. The biggest players in fashion worked for improved working conditions, safety regulations, and even higher wages for workers. We cleverly managed the additional costs of these improvements by simply cutting corners on the quality of the final products. After all, an outfit that was barely going to be worn doesn't need to be particularly well made.

For a time, it looked like the patch would hold. The workers were getting a much better deal, consumers could still feed their unquenchable thirst for novelty, and we were making record profits. Under the surface, trouble was brewing. There were certainly lots of reasons: the scrutiny over the growing income gap here and abroad, increased publicity about the effects of climate change, and efforts by the manufacturing countries to move beyond poverty level economies. But I suspect the two major factors were the growing voice of the women's movement combined with the transparency of our new age of citizen journalism. As more and more social media posts and YouTube documentaries circulated showcasing the plight of a largely female workforce, it became ever more difficult for even the most rabid consumer to not see a ghost of exploitation when they looked in the mirror.

All these issues fueled the rise of a small but increasingly public movement to embrace sustainable fashion. The main tactics in those early days were to slow down the churn of clothing from factory to closet to landfill with recycling and reuse. Some of the leading names in the fashion industry were early converts, but beyond the celebrity appeal there was little practical impact on the overall business.

Then Mother Nature stepped in and changed everything. Who would have imagined that a couple damn typhoons could crash a worldwide industry? But they did. The 2022 typhoon season was the worst on record. Storms devastated the clothing factories in Vietnam and Bangladesh. Within a couple of months more than 60 percent of the world's production capacity was gone. The tree huggers called it karma.

The biggest clothing labels saw it as a sign that it was time to join the environmental movement. The economics made perfect sense. At the time, the most popular form of recycled clothing used fibers made from old plastic. By the early 2020s, even with growing efforts to ban some plastics, we were still throwing away enough every year to circle the earth four times. Most of it ultimately ended up in the oceans where it congealed into massive islands of trash. All we had to do was scoop it up. It was like we had discovered a virtually inexhaustible goldmine of raw materials. Plus, the optics were brilliant. You could have your cool clothes and help the environment all at the same time. Environmentalism that was profitable. It was a win-win that promised to make some people, like me, even richer.

We rushed to build new factories, most of them state of the art, using the latest in robotics to replace the human labor. Fast Fashion 2.0 was just about to explode when the second stiletto dropped.

This one was a dagger through the heart of the industry. It turned out that clothes made from recycled plastic shed microscopic plastic fibers each time they were washed. We were scooping up millions of tons of plastics from the oceans only to replace them with trillions of tiny particles that were far more dangerous. Once the news started to spread on social media, the reaction was swift.

At first, I couldn't believe how fast consumers walked away from the traditional manufacturers. Looking back now, it is obvious that the community-based fashion movement had quietly been spreading from the fringes to main street. Because these new designers and makers were small, they had managed to remain below our radar. They combined their ability to connect digitally with an astute understanding of how to build a local following. When the crisis hit, they stepped in and replaced a model that had been thriving since the birth of the industrial revolution. Their success was proof that change can happen virtually overnight when the right forces are aligned.

Collaborative makers' spaces that were already springing up in communities became the new craft clothing factories. Individual designers built businesses that served local clientele and won national fame. Closets began to empty out as people bought clothing with purpose and durability.

Now it seems we have come full circle, to a world where the artisans once again dominate the fashion marketplace—where the value of a piece of clothing is no longer based on its newness, but on how many times it can be reimagined and reused. An old idea has been reborn using the new tools of the digital age and fueled by individual empowerment. It seems that those ubiquitous T-shirts have helped to create a new form of capitalism that many people believe will prove to be more resilient than anything we had tried before.

4

Reimagining Automation

Elvis Ivanovich, Robot-Lover

The marchers were already gathering on the street as Elvis rode into work. Most were milling around, clutching cups of coffee to ward off the chill of an unexpected late freeze. Steam rose from their cupped hands and framed mostly white, mostly male faces. Once proud, they were now the last of a disappearing breed.

At the head of the disorganized line, a handful of men was trying to form some semblance of organization. These were the leaders of the ARL, the Anti-Robot League. Elvis had known many of them for most of his life, worked next to them, and shared beers with them at union cookouts back in the day. Once they had been his friends. Now, most of them considered him the enemy. Some of these very men had even threatened him on that fateful day. He would never forget the rage and anger on their faces.

He didn't fear them anymore or return their anger. They were scared then, and they're still scared today. Seeing them made him sad. Sad that they could only see a bleak, hopeless future. Sad that if he passed any of them on the street, they would still look the other way. Sad that many still saw him as a traitor.

In a strange way, he owed them all a debt. Five years ago, at the height of their rage, they had lashed out. Through no fault of his own, he had been in the path of that anger. His simple act that day had changed the course of his life. Every year since then, he had to relive the event. The video of that scene had become as much a staple of the May Day news streams as their ragged march down main streets across the country. This year, there would be one difference. This year, Elvis would add a new chapter to that story, one that he believed could help convince even the most hardened members of the ARL that the future did not have to be so dark.

The day that started this whole chain of events had begun just like any other. Elvis left home early and drove to the plant where he had worked for more than ten years. When he arrived, he pulled into the vast empty parking lot. He could have parked right next to the entrance in one of the many spots that had once been reserved for the most senior employees. He chose instead, like he always did, the spot he had been assigned when he had started as an apprentice maintenance engineer. Back then the lot would have been full, and Elvis would have walked to the plant, greeting his co-workers and making small talk. Today, he hustled toward the employee entrance alone, head bent against the wind that whipped across the empty lot.

The entrance led directly to the employee locker room. Inside, the workers had once gathered to store their personal items or grab a quick cup of coffee before starting their shifts. Today, the hundreds of lockers sat empty. Out of habit, Elvis continued to use the same one he always had. He changed into the clean room overalls the company required him to wear as quickly as he could. The locker room was the one place where he felt most alone.

All those abandoned lockers reminded him of the hundreds of people who had lost everything when management announced they were going to fully automate the plant. Somehow being here alone made Elvis feel complicit with this decision. He knew it wasn't his fault. He certainly hadn't taken away all the jobs, or even lobbied to be one of the skeleton crew kept on to train the robots that replaced the workers.

Management had been circumspect about how they had chosen the lucky few who would remain for this transition period. There had been rumors that Elvis and the dozen others had been selected based on personality profiles. Supposedly, HR believed they would be the ones most likely to adapt to the new circumstances of working with robots. Those who harangued him on the street, his former co-workers, had a different view. Many of them believed it was because Elvis was spineless, afraid to stand up to the bosses. They had taken to calling him robot-lover behind his back.

Elvis didn't consider himself a particularly courageous person, but he suspected that the real explanation for his selection was far less dramatic. He had been working as a maintenance engineer long enough to understand the job, but he was still at a junior pay grade. In short, he was the best, cheapest, alternative. At least believing that made him feel better than thinking himself a traitor.

Dressed in his clean suit and wearing the tracking device that monitored his location and his vital signs, he left the locker room and headed for the main floor. On this day, he didn't give much thought to the hundreds of robot arms, in all sizes and shapes, that were performing a silent ballet across the plant. He hardly even noticed the smaller autonomous robots that scurried across the floor on their way to perform important errands that once were the province of human workers.

Elvis's job was to help train the autonomous maintenance robots that had replaced his fellow workers. These duties had been explained to him by the head of the programming team, a young woman named Maggie, on the first day of his new job. The meeting had taken place in her office, high above the plant floor. From her perch, she could monitor the activities of all the robots and their human trainers. She had struck him as the kind of person who would watch over them closely.

"We've programmed the AMBots for every piece of equipment in the facility with step-by-step instructions from the service manuals. Each robot has access to over 10,000 pages of repair instructions. They're designed to diagnose the problem, match it to the correct repair instructions, and implement the repair," she had explained.

Elvis couldn't help but snicker when he heard this.

"Something wrong?" Her demeanor suddenly turned icy.

"Sorry, no . . . " Elvis stammered, "it's just when a new guy comes on the maintenance team they give them those manuals and tell them good luck. It's kind of like a hazing. Most of the repair instructions make no sense or are plain wrong."

"And that's why you have a job now." She made sure to emphasize the now, reminding him that his position was temporary at best. "We need you to monitor the AMBots' work. When you see that they are following a procedure that isn't going to result in resolution, you alert us. In most cases, we'll be able to reprogram the unit in real time."

"What if the correct procedure isn't the fastest or easiest solution? Do you want to know about those too?" he asked, innocently.

It took her a moment to respond, as if the question had never occurred to her. "It could be useful for you to note those as well. We'll keep them on file and review them later. For this first phase, our goal is simply to make sure the procedural programming is correct. We'll look at improving AMBot efficiency in subsequent phases."

With that, she had dismissed Elvis. Her assistant escorted him downstairs to the factory floor where he met his team for the first time. Elvis was assigned to monitor five identical robots. Each was about three feet tall and had six wheels. His first thought was that they looked more like mini-fridges than replacements for a team of experienced maintenance engineers. The only things that made them look at all like what Elvis expected were the four spindly arms and one round cyclops-like video eye.

He quickly learned that looks were deceiving. The first surprise came when they started moving. Each wheel was independently mounted and powered by a servomotor. The little buggers were fast and incredibly nimble.

They could maneuver into the tightest spaces and easily extend their bodies up to a height of nine feet. The arms could also extend out to four feet on all sides. When they were fully extended and working on one of the big robots, they reminded Elvis a little of Lenny, one of his former colleagues. Lenny was six foot six, skinny as a rail, and had the longest arms Elvis had ever seen. He was the one who got called whenever the repair was in one of the many tight spaces along the line. Now Elvis was babysitting an entire team of robotic Lennies.

It quickly became apparent that this wasn't going to be the do-nothing job he had imagined. From the first day, the robots ran into problems as they tried to perform their tasks without wavering from the step-by-step instructions of their programming. Elvis had to step in repeatedly and alert the designers that the robots had hit a wall. He would then send the programmers a set of revised instructions and wait for them to reprogram the robots.

Despite the promise from Maggie that these changes could be made "in real time," Elvis would often have to sit and wait for an hour or more for even the simplest corrections. The whole time, he would be thinking that if he only had his tools he could just make the repair and the factory would be back up and running. More than once he caught himself imagining that the Lennies looked just as bored as he felt.

As he stepped out onto the main factory floor, he checked his wristpad. It looked like the first assignment for today was replacing a control unit on one of the big robot welding arms. It was a process that the Lennies had done often enough that they had it pretty much down. Still, the electronics in the control unit were delicate and had to be handled carefully. He hurried off to join them.

The robot team had almost completed the repair when the protesters broke into the factory. Elvis was so absorbed in watching his little team that he didn't hear the commotion as two dozen former workers burst out of the employee locker room. They carried sledgehammers and had already smashed the few unfortunate robots in their path before they came upon Elvis and his team.

He was so startled to see other humans in the plant that, at first, he didn't process what they were doing. "What are . . . you can't be here," he said.

"Bullshit," an older man at the front of the group responded. As soon as he spoke, Elvis recognized him. He had been a senior maintenance engineer and now was the leader of the newly formed anti-robot league, or ARL for short.

He continued, "We belong here. It's them damn things that don't have any right to be here."

The others behind him muttered in agreement, and the entire group took a few steps toward Elvis.

Elvis turned to check on the bots. By now the factory sensors had registered the intruders, and the bots had all stopped working. They looked helpless, gathered behind Elvis, as if they were looking to him for protection. He doubted their programming included how to defend themselves against a mob intent on bashing them to pieces.

He turned back toward the men. “This won’t bring your jobs back.”

The leader’s face turned dark red with anger. “Get out of our way—or else.”

Elvis took a deep breath and tried to muster up his courage. He looked the leader square in the eye and quietly replied, “No.” He clenched his fists by his side and prepared himself for what would happen next.

Elvis and the protesters stood like that, while all around them the machines in the factory stood frozen. Elvis could feel a bead of sweat start to roll down his forehead. Even as it slid into his eye and blurred his vision, he willed himself not to blink.

The only movement that was taking place was out of sight of Elvis. The plant security team had detected the protesters even before they entered the building and were on their way. Management had been warned of a possible attack by disgruntled employees. The security team was heavily armed with stun guns.

The leader of the protesters considered Elvis. “Last chance. Get out of our way.”

Elvis didn’t move, barely even breathing.

“Your choice. Boys, move him out.”

Two of the group took a couple steps toward Elvis. Before they could reach him, the security team rushed in from all sides, surrounding the protesters. The leader of the mob rushed the security officer closest to him, hammer raised high in the air. He was nowhere near to landing a blow before the officer took him down with his stunner. As the leader lay twitching on the floor, the rest of the group realized that they were outnumbered and outgunned.

"Put down your weapons and get down on your knees. Hands behind your heads. Now!" The security team leader barked out the orders.

After a moment of confusion, the protesters complied. The officers moved in and quickly cuffed them.

As the protesters were being led away, the security team leader approached Elvis. "Are you okay?"

"Yeah, fine."

"You need to report to the office then."

Elvis turned to check on the robots, still huddled behind him, "But what about—" He stopped before finishing the question. The robots would be fine without him.

As he was walking across the still motionless plant floor, he noticed the vid drones following him for the first time. Some were part of the company security system, but at least a couple looked like media drones. He wondered how much of the scene they had recorded.

He found out the answer before he left the factory that day. The entire "attack," as it was being called, was on all the live streams. Most were replaying the scene of him standing up to the protesters, protecting the robots, over and over.

The online pundits were consumed with trying to unravel his motivation. Some praised him as a man simply doing his job; a throwback to a time when honor mattered. Others were less charitable and labeled him a shill for management, a robot-lover lackey.

Of course, they all wanted to hear from him. His message feed was blowing up with requests for interviews, statements, invitations to appear on every vlog in the webiverse, it seemed.

He deleted them all and went home, where he stayed hidden for the rest of the week. By then, the mediasphere had lost interest in his motivations and the story in general. But he still couldn't have answered their question: "Why did he stand up for the robots?" It would take him many more weeks before he completely sorted that one out. In the meantime, he had to deal with the immediate blow-back from his decision.

Even after the media lost interest, his neighbors were not so forgiving. He had already been shunned because he was one of the lucky ones who kept his job. Now he could hardly walk down the street without getting glares from people he had once called his friends. He lost count of the number of times he was called robot-lover or worse when he was out on the street. Angela, his longtime girlfriend, moved out of the apartment and refused to speak to him.

It was, without a doubt, the worst time of his life. The one bright spot was work. The plant had offered him as much time off as he needed but he was back on the job the next week. Things at the plant quickly got back to normal. For the next couple of weeks, Elvis and his Lennies fell back into their routine.

Then one day, he got a surprise visit from the owner of the robotics company, Mr. Mark Marcone, a middle-aged man with the quiet bearing of an engineer. Nothing about him suggested that he was on a mission to destroy the livelihoods of all the people who had once worked at the plant.

He arrived on the floor surrounded by a bevy of assistants. Marcone ignored them all and made Elvis feel like the only person there. He peppered Elvis with questions about his work with the robots for nearly twenty minutes before dropping his bombshell. The robotics company was giving Elvis a $50,000 bonus for protecting the robots from the protesters. When he told Elvis the amount, he joked that now Elvis could buy his own robot.

After Marcone and his entourage had left, Elvis found himself back in the comforting silence of the plant. The Lennies were working on a repair that should have been simple, but they were making little progress. Reluctantly, he stopped them and sent new instructions to the programmers. While he waited for them to reprogram the robots, he tried to process what had just happened. It felt like a stroke of good fortune, maybe enough to help mend the riff with Angela. The more he thought about it, the more excited he got. Surely this would bring them back together? He tried calling to tell her the good news. She didn't pick-up, so he sent her a long text explaining what had happened.

Her curt response came back almost immediately. It read: I HAVE NO USE FOR YOUR ROBOT-LOVER BLOOD MONEY. LEAVE ME ALONE!

He stood there, stunned. How had this happened? He played back the past few weeks of his life, wondering how it could have been different? What if he had stepped aside and let the ARL destroy the robots? What if he had refused the job in the first place? Would any of it have made a difference?

Try as hard as he could, Elvis couldn't convince himself that different actions on his part would have really mattered. Oh sure, Angela might still be in his life. His friends wouldn't have abandoned him. They could all stew in their anger and rage against what the owners of the plant called progress. He couldn't see how any of those choices would alter the course of the future.

That night, as he paced around his apartment, he struggled to make sense of the entire series of events he had been swept up in.

What could Elvis Ivanovich, simple maintenance engineer, do that would have any impact beyond his own life? How could his voice matter?

The next morning, bleary-eyed from lack of sleep, Elvis returned to work. Preoccupied with questions from the night before, he mindlessly went through his routine. When he arrived on the plant floor, the robots were sitting motionless, waiting for another set of updated instructions to be sent down from the programmers in the office high above them.

Suddenly, the answer was clear to him. He went straight to Maggie's office. When he entered, she was peering over the shoulder of one of the coders working intently. Maggie's shoulders were clenched tightly as she continually looked from the coder's screen to her wristpad to check the time.

Elvis stood just inside the doorway, trying to get up the nerve to speak. Finally, he managed. "Excuse me, Ma'am."

Startled, Maggie turned and looked around the room. Her eyes locked on Elvis, and she stared at him with an expression that made it clear that now was not the time to interrupt her.

"What?" she snapped.

"That's my Lenny you're working on," he struggled to get the line out without stammering.

"Lenny?!" she demanded.

"Sorry," he blushed, "That's just what I call them. Anyway, I think you guys are going at this all wrong." He took a deep breath. There, he had said it.

"We're kind of busy right now Mr. Ivanovich." Maggie turned away with such force that Elvis thought she might lose her balance and fall.

She muttered to the coder. "Get those damn things working."

"Busy doing work that you don't have to do," Elvis blurted it out.

Maggie flinched but refused to turn around. "I suppose you have a better idea?" The sarcasm in her voice was intended to make him go away.

It didn't work. Instead, Elvis paused to take a deep breath and then stepped into the office. "Yes ma'am, I think I do. See, the problem is that you want to suck all the experience and knowledge out of my brain and stuff it in the Lenny—I mean robot. But there is no way to ever do that." As he continued to explain, he walked toward Maggie and the coder, unconsciously trying to will her to turn and listen to him.

"Instead of trying to replace human workers with robots, what if we worked together? The Lennies can do some things better than I could ever do, and there are other things a person with experience will always be able to do better. They have strength and flexibility, but we've got intuition. Together we could keep this plant running 100 percent of the time." By the time he had finished his speech, he was standing so close that she could feel his breath on her neck.

Maggie whipped around, her face just inches away from his. Startled, Elvis leaned away but refused to step back. He had come this far; he wasn't going to give up.

Maggie gave him her best condescending stare and spoke slowly as if talking to a dimwitted child. "Mr. Ivanovich, this is a multi-million-dollar project. Our goal here is much, much bigger than just fixing a few broken machines. We're demonstrating the feasibility of the universal autonomous factory. I can understand, given recent events, how you might feel bad for your fellow workers, but this is not a jobs program."

The two stared at each other. The standoff was broken by the coder announcing, "New program uploaded."

In that moment, they both knew that Elvis had lost the battle. Maggie smiled in triumph and turned her back on him.

"Mr. Ivanovich, I believe we need you back down on the floor. That is, if you want to continue working here."

Without another word, Elvis turned and left the office, but he didn't go back down to the plant floor. Instead, he went straight to Human Resources where he submitted his resignation, effective immediately. The confused, but sympathetic, HR rep asked what he intended to do next.

Elvis replied with a smile, "Buy myself a robot."

The next year flew by in a blur. Elvis was so busy starting up his new company that he hardly noticed that only a few of his old friends had even asked why he quit. Those who did chided him for giving up a good-paying job. He didn't try to explain his reasons, assuming they wouldn't begin to understand.

Elvis did find people who believed in his plan when he connected with the local open source robotics community. There, he met a couple of robot designers who were thrilled to join him. The goal was simple: they would design a general purpose autonomous collaborative robot or cobot.

The cobot would use artificial intelligence to learn by observing its human partner. Ultimately the goal was for robot and human to work as a team. Together, they could perform maintenance in a factory, care for the elderly in a nursing home, or even run the kitchen in a gourmet restaurant. They decided to name their robot Robbie after one of the most famous robots in science fiction.

Even with the help of the open source community, the challenge of actually building the first prototype exhausted all of Elvis's capital. After months of hard work, it looked as if Robbie would be an unrealized dream.

Elvis and his small team were sitting in the tiny space they had rented at the local maker's lab. The Robbie prototype sat quietly in the corner, as Elvis explained that he had run out of funds and unless someone had a brilliant idea they would have to shut down.

Jess, one of the youngest designers on the team, spoke up first. "Why don't we crowdfund?

Elvis threw his hands up in despair. "I've never raised money before. I wouldn't know how to start."

Jess tapped his wristpad and an image of a webpage called Britbots appeared above the table. "It's really simple. This platform has been around for nearly twenty years and it's specifically for people looking to raise funds for robot projects."

As he continued to talk, Jess swiped through a series of pages displaying an amazing assortment of projects, ranging from robotic toys and tutors to deep sea explorers.

Elvis considered the images. "You think anyone would really want to invest in our idea?"

"Oh, hell yeah," Jess exclaimed. "Think about it, man. We're building a robot to give average people a chance to be part of the robotics revolution. Anyone who invests now will be one of the first to become part of this new owner class."

Elvis had to admit it was an exciting idea—one he hadn't completely thought through, but he realized, at the very worst, it was better than giving up.

Within a few days they had the crowdfunding site launched. It went slowly at first, but by the end of the month they were attracting serious investments. In six weeks they had met their funding goal.

They raised enough money to keep working and expand the company. They rented an old warehouse space and hired new employees. They even brought on a marketing team. At the first meeting in their new space, Elvis announced their goal: "In less than eighteen months we are going to launch our fully autonomous cobot for the general marketplace. Robbie will be no more expensive than an automobile was just a decade ago. For the first time, almost anyone will have the chance to own the means of production. Our product is going to revolutionize the way we think about work, automation, and ownership."

The new employees had tons of questions but none more important than the actual launch date. Elvis thought for the briefest of moments before he circled a day in red on the giant wall calendar. May 1st, May Day, 2033.

The PR team went crazy when they heard this. They knew that releasing Robbie on the same day that Anti-Robot League demonstrators were protesting would send clicks totally off the charts.

The date was arbitrarily ambitious. Meeting it meant that everyone in the small factory had to work incredible hours for the next eighteen months. Now the day was here.

The Waymo-Lyft dropped Elvis off at the entrance to the nondescript warehouse that served as the headquarters for Collaborative Robots Unlimited. He was greeted in the lobby by the floating screens streaming the day's news. There it was again, the video of Elvis standing between the mob and the Lennies. The commentator was talking about how Elvis Ivanovich, the famous robot-lover, would be announcing a new product today. She went on to speculate that he would undoubtedly be asked what was going through his mind when he stood up to the angry mob.

Elvis smiled as he watched the scene. At least this time he would have an answer to that question. He could now finally show the world that robots and humans could work together. Then one day, he hoped, everyone would become a robot lover.

Archie's Apology

Of course, automation eliminates jobs. That's the whole point, isn't it? Since the beginning of the industrial age, we've found ways to improve productivity and cut costs by substituting labor-saving technology for humans.

When the advances in robotics finally started to catch up with the hype it seemed like we were finally on the verge of realizing our dream of owning all parts of the production process—even the workers. Workers who never needed a break, or healthcare, or even lights and heat for that matter.

Oh, I know so many people talked about how unfair it was to the workers. But we had plenty of data on our side that told us that for every job eliminated by technology, at least two new ones were created. Maybe that didn't help the factory worker who found himself unskilled and out of a job, but it kept the overall economy in balance. And that was our job, maintain the balance.

How could we have known it was going to be different this time? As technology replaced more and more workers, the new jobs did appear just as we had expected. But they were quickly taken by the next generation of automation. Still, we pressed on, secure in our belief that the system would self-correct. I began to suspect we had misanalysed the situation when the talk turned to a future filled with completely autonomous companies, everyone from the workers on the plant floor to the CEO replaced by some form of artificial intelligence! If the machines could replace even me, what did that mean for the future of humanity?

It turned out that the system did find a way to self-correct, just not with us still in charge. The shift began with the education system. We had carefully managed public education to meet our needs for a constant and willing supply of workers skilled to perform the specific work we required, and little more. When our needs changed, from factory workers to office drones, the system was designed to adapt. During most of the twentieth century, it did a pretty good job of keeping up with those changes.

When we began to replace more and more jobs with machines, software, and even artificial intelligence, the old approach to education became less and less relevant. Before the business community fully recognized this, a few of the more forward-thinking institutions shifted their focus. They slowly moved from chasing next year's skillset to enhancing uniquely human talents. By teaching creativity, critical thinking, and entrepreneurial skills, they built a workforce better prepared to weather a world of accelerated technological obsolescence. As it turned out, that workforce was also better able to shape the future than we could have ever hoped to be.

They challenged the myth that industrial automation would inevitably take over all work. They argued that we humans had the right and power to set whatever boundaries we needed.

Fear of unchecked automation caused a public backlash. Public sentiment spawned a market for products labeled NORO, no robots. Of course, they didn't represent an economically viable option. We flooded the markets with cheaper and cheaper products made in our automated factories. Imagine our surprise when some consumers willingly chose to pay more to support their fellow workers.

The robotics companies realized that their existence was threatened if this clash became a full-scale war. They saw a possible third way and began designing robots to collaborate, not replace. These new cobots enhanced profits and productivity while creating new and unexpected opportunities for workers.

The first robot owner's co-op was an experiment in social welfare. A group of nonprofits came up with the radical idea of former workers owning and leasing out their personal robots. The first time we heard that one, we had a good laugh. At the time, most robots were expensive and not particularly portable. Robot owning co-ops indeed!

Once again, our self-importance blinded us to the changes that were taking place. Robots quickly spread beyond large-scale factories and started showing up everywhere; from hospitals to fast food joints. Suddenly, personal ownership didn't seem so far-fetched.

With funding from nonprofits, crowdsourcing, and even some government incentives, a new business model began to grow. It took off when the big robotics companies saw the opportunity to sell to a new customer. Robot dealerships began to appear, often taking over the showrooms of abandoned car dealerships. Anyone could walk in, pick the latest model, and arrange financing on the spot. Buying your first robot has become a rite of passage as common as buying that first car had been in the last century. In the process, the exclusive owners' club has been blown apart.

5

Reimagining the Gig Economy

Andy and Sue Plan Their Getaway

"Hey, Boss—sorry to interrupt, but it's time."

Andy was so engrossed in the painting she was working on that it took her a moment to realize that the voice was talking to her. She leaned back and considered the canvas. An arid wasteland rendered in bright neon colors. Rusting hulks of abandoned automobiles litter what is left of the Pacific Coast Highway. It is the background for Andy's latest VR project, an afro-cyberpunk reimagining of Octavia Butler's Earthseed stories. She live-streamed her painting sessions to her nearly 2 million followers. They could watch the VR come to life in real time, as Andy designed everything from the settings to the characters.

Working this way, she could build an audience for her projects as they developed. By the time she was ready to release, there would already be a substantial fan base anxiously waiting for the new project. Andy wasn't the only VR designer to work live, but she was one of the few who designed old school, using paint and canvas. Her works always created quite the buzz among fans of historical romance VRs, and the finished paintings were a nice income stream.

She rubbed her eyes. "Wow, Lacey, is it already 3:00?"

Lacey responded with a laugh, "More like 5:45."

"You let me work that long?"

"You seemed to have some serious flow going on. I didn't want to interrupt. So, I just rearranged the afternoon to give you max time," Lacey explained.

"Thanks."

"Just doing my job, Boss. And now you should have just enough time to take a short break before the Rodríguez meeting."

Andy rose from her seat and crossed the small, cluttered studio. As she walked, she stretched to work out the kinks from the hours spent in intense concentration. Her eyes roamed across the dozens of different projects in varying stages of completion. They ranged from computer screens covered in complex mathematical calculations to hand-built art objects. Andy thrived on the chaos. She would shift seamlessly from one project to the next, often working on as many as six or seven different ones throughout the day. She found that when she was deeply engrossed in one project, she often had unexpected insights about another. When an epiphany struck, she would drop what she was doing to capture the moment.

Of course, that kind of creative freedom could have its downside since Andy's projects were her livelihood. Keeping Andy focused and making sure that projects got done on time was Lacey's job. Well, one of Lacey's jobs. As personal virtual assistant to Andy and her partner Suzie, Lacey was responsible for coordinating Andy's work, running the house, and managing their social calendars. Suzie had a separate smart agent for work. She preferred the separation.

This was an idea that Andy couldn't really understand. For her, the boundaries between work and private life had dissolved more than a decade ago, about the same time that she had met Suzie.

She'd been gig-hopping as an experimental mathematician at the time. Not a particularly lucrative income stream but she had an unusually high aptitude for esoteric math. It did lead to some interesting projects, like the one she worked on with Suzie; an early Mars prototype mission for Space X. Suzie was the triber for the project. It was her job to source, hire, and manage the gig-hoppers brought on for mega-projects funded by venture groups or virtual corporations. She was part HR department, part CFO, and part mother/confessor to the teams.

When the project was completed, everyone would go their separate ways. They might work together on the next project, or again in a few years, or never. Andy had made a point of staying in touch with Suzie. In the beginning, she had told herself it was just to get future work. To be honest, she had been crushing on Suzie since the first week they worked together. It didn't take long for work chats to turn into meeting for drinks, dinner, and dates. It was a whirlwind romance, and both were surprised when they decided to move in together after just a few months. Now they were about to celebrate their tenth anniversary together.

Andy opened the door and stepped into the garden. The warm sun caused her to pause and take a deep breath, inhaling the rich fragrance of flowers, herbs, and designer botanicals precisely selected to stimulate her neural receptors. As she crossed the garden, she paused next to a container filled with young spinach. The plants had a faint iridescent glow, as if someone had put nanoLEDs around the leaves. They glowed because of a genetic hack that made them emit light as they neared their peak nutritional value. Different plants even had different color schemes to indicate which nutrients were most active. At night, the soft glow of the plants made the garden look like a magical world. Suzie had once said that she expected to see little pixies flittering around. Andy had been working on that project for the past couple of months as an anniversary gift for Suzie. Andy was pretty sure she would love them; tiny drones that looked like living fairies and lit up like fireflies as they flew.

Andy picked a handful of spinach. She left the leaves that were glowing the brightest for Suzie. She was going to need all the antioxidants she could get when she got home from work. Suzie only worked on the biggest and most complex projects. She had made quite the name for herself tribeing everything from space launches to geoengineering. Andy understood her partner's motivation; she just didn't think it was worth the stress of physically commuting every day.

Since the early days of telework, there had been a never-ending debate over the productivity of working remotely versus in an office environment. The consensus tended to swing back and forth, depending on the latest research study from Watson, but the general trend had been moving consistently toward remote work. These days, few professionals spent more than 10 percent of their time working in a shared space. There were exceptions—projects that were extremely complex, or that used a company's most vital intel and needed to make sure the data was kept secure. It was a lot easier to protect vital data with all the players in one secure offline space versus monitoring a bunch of lone giggers sitting in coffee shops all over the world. Andy knew that for her, the advantages of working alone far outweighed the downsides.

It wasn't that Andy was antisocial. She needed human interaction and got plenty of it during her workday. Most of her meetings happened in VR, but the technology had advanced so much that it was impossible to distinguish the experience from being in the same space. Plus, she had Lacey as her constant companion.

Lacey was waiting for her in the kitchen. Well, on the refrigerator screen at least. In a world where most interactions were mediated, talking with your assistant via kitchen appliance was commonplace. There was certainly nothing about Lacey's beautiful Indian features and slightly exotic accent to suggest she was anything less than a real human being. She could have been in the next room or in Mumbai. Of course, she was in neither place but resided, so to speak, in the cloud where she could oversee all the house's systems.

Most of the time she communicated with Andy and Suzie as a disembodied voice. They had grown up with voice-activated smart agents, so this was more normal to them than picking up a telephone to have a conversation. Like most people their age, they had accepted the fully realized video avatars as soon as the technology was available. It turns out that humans still like to see who they are talking to, at least occasionally. Those moments weren't random. Lacey was programmed to sense when Andy was feeling isolated and needed visual interaction.

"So, Boss, I was thinking a mean greenie smoothie?"

"Sounds good," Andy replied as she opened the refrigerator.

Lacey had already loaded the smoothie recipe to the frig. The ingredients she needed were highlighted by the nanoLEDs embedded in their containers.

"Looks like we're out of maqui, so I substituted blueberries. Do you want me to put in a special order or just add it to the regular delivery?

"Regular order is fine. Thanks, Lacey."

Andy gathered the ingredients, tossed them in the blender. A few minutes later she was sitting in the garden, enjoying her smoothie with the warm sun on her face.

Lacey interrupted her reverie. "Boss, you've got just enough time to do a walk-through before your meeting."

Andy responded with a laugh, "Lacey you are a slave driver."

"Just doing my job."

Andy finished her smoothie and headed to the room they dubbed the *holodeck*. The dimly lit ten-by-ten space looked more like an empty storage room than a set from a long ago sci-fi show.

Andy slipped on her VR glasses and gloves. She blinked twice to activate the system and was immersed in a photorealistic version of the house she was designing for her clients. The illusion was indistinguishable from reality. The resolution was just right—not so perfect to reveal that this was a CGI render. The gloves provided the sensation of feel when she touched anything, or anyone, sharing the space with her.

She did a quick walkthrough of the house to make sure everything was just right for the meeting. The house was small by last century standards, but Andy knew every trick to make it felt spacious and inviting. The key feature was the great room with its wall of glass that provided a view of the lush garden she imagined would one day fill the courtyard. Like most of Andy's designs the glass was functional as well as beautiful. Microscopic filaments in the glass would generate enough electricity to meet all the homeowners' needs.

The room was almost perfect but needed just a tiny tweak. She swiped her hand across the scene and pulled in one of the side walls, altering the vista.

"Better. Now for some wall swag," she thought out loud. She called up options from one of her favorite designers. The inventory of framed art, mirrors, and wall hangings that appeared were all upcycled from industrial salvage. She swiped through a half-dozen before she came to an oversized mirror with a sleek metallic frame. She positioned it on the wall opposite her.

Suddenly a man in his mid-forties was staring back at her from the mirror. She stepped back, startled. The man mimicked her movement.

"Wow, so that's what the Rodríguez's imagine I look like," she chuckled.

She had forgotten that they were older and likely used preference filtering. Instead of interacting with Andy's regular avatar, who looked almost exactly like Andy—an Amerasian woman in her late forties, medium height, with deep blue eyes—they saw someone who fit their preconceived image of the perfect architect. He was consistent with all the personal data she had downloaded about the clients when the project had first started. At least he had her blue eyes.

Many of her older clients did the same thing. It was one of the reasons that she went by her gender-neutral nickname instead of her given name: Aneko. It was no problem when her involvement in a project was all virtual. Although, there had been a few embarrassing moments in real space when she had to introduce herself to her clients at their housewarming party.

The doorbell chimed. Andy crossed to the entrance foyer to greet Mr. and Ms. Rodríguez. It would be their first time touring the house. She hoped they liked the work.

Half an hour later the conference ended with the Rodríguez's blown away by the *maravilloso* work done by their favorite architect. Just a few minor changes and she could hand the project off to the 3-D printers. Nice to get that one behind her, she thought as she removed the glasses and stepped out of the small room.

Loud music was pumping from the exercise room down the hall. Suzie must have gotten home and started her workout. Andy could tell from her choice of soundtrack that she had a lot of stress to work off. She decided to change and join her.

By the time Andy got changed, the workout music had been replaced by a softly droning meditation audio. Andy entered to find Suzie sitting cross-legged, with her eyes closed. She could see from the serene look on her face that the exercise had done the trick. She smiled as she admired her partner. Her skin was the color of dark honey, and her perfectly symmetrical features were framed by the tumble of her long dark, luxurious hair. Andy couldn't believe how lucky she was to have found the perfect soul mate, at work no less. She couldn't resist the urge to give her a quick kiss on the top of the head before sitting down across from her and closing her eyes. They sat like that, for the next half-hour, as the rhythm of their breathing became one.

The singing bowl rang out to signal the end of the session.

"Hi, Lover," Andy said as she opened her eyes. "How was your day at the office?"

"Ugh," was Suzie's response. "One I'd like to forget."

Andy stood up. She pulled Suzie from the floor and into her arms. "I can help with that," she whispered.

"Oh, what did you have in mind?" Suzie asked teasingly.

"Lacey and I have been working on some ideas for our anniversary vacation. Wanna see?"

Suzie sighed and pulled away. "There better be wine with this, Lacey, if you two are going to convince me to travel. You know how much I hate to travel. All I want to do is take a nice long VirCation."

"The vacation previews are ready to be viewed in the den. Wine is chilled and waiting," Lacey offered.

"We've got lots of options. Even some that don't require you to leave our bed, I promise. C'mon it'll be fun," Andy said as she grabbed Suzie by the hand. "Let's just agree to go into it with an open mind."

By the end of the evening, they'd finished off the bottle of wine and previewed more than two dozen possible vacations. Andy had been telling the truth. With Lacey's help, she had amassed a wildly imaginative set of possibilities. The options ranged from virtual historical romance tours to a virtual Burning Man raver set on the moon. The *real* options included everything from mountain hiking in Tanzania to a luxury arctic cruise.

Making a final decision had taken some good-natured back and forth as Lacey worked to refine the offerings to satisfy them both. They finally settled on a trip to a remote island in the Indian Ocean. The resort was beautiful and isolated. Once there they could retreat to a private bungalow over the water and not see anyone but each other.

"It is beautiful." Suzie agreed. "If only someone would invent teleportation, so we didn't have to go through the hassle of travel."

"Hum, maybe I could work on the math for that," Andy mused. "But in the meantime, it won't be so bad. Air Maroc owes me a couple of business class flights for all the work I've done for them. We have plenty of carbon credits for the trip, one advantage of working from home. We'll snuggle into one of their couple's pods, slip into a great VR, and you won't know you've even left the house."

"I hear that they have a very talented VR designer." Suzie laughed and kissed Andy.

Lacey dimmed the lights.

Archie's Apology

This may come as a surprise, but being a job creator can be pretty damn stressful. Oh, sure, there is a real ego boost to be able to brag that tens of thousands of people rely on you for their very survival. Even if most of your employees hate you, they will treat you like royalty and jump to do just about anything you demand. But, oh man—what a hassle it is having employees. Beyond just having to make sure the companies are profitable, there are all the rules on how you have to treat people, provide benefits, pay taxes . . . and don't even get me started on pensions and retirement funds. I can't tell you the number of times I sat around with other CEOs and we dreamed about how wonderful it would be to have a business without employees.

Then these new entities like Uber came on the scene and showed it was possible to run a business totally staffed by independent contractors. Well, we were jealous, to put it mildly. Not so much for their technology but for the fact that they had the cojones to say out loud what we all believed: you shouldn't be obligated to your employees just because you made a profit.

Of course, Uber wasn't the first, and they ran into an awful lot of problems. Their missteps fooled many people into believing this new gig economy—where full-time workers were replaced by temps and contractors—wouldn't take off. What most people didn't realize was that it already had. Between 2000 and 2020, 90 percent of the new jobs created in this country were temporary positions.

Our ability to collect and use real-time data made it possible to predict the ebb and flow of work at a micro-level we never had before. With that kind of knowledge, it didn't matter if you were running a factory or a fast-food joint, it was easy to create just-in-time labor. No more paying employees to stand around. This move was a boon to the bottom line. It was like our wildest dreams had come true.

It wasn't just about greed. Our system privileged the obsessive pursuit of productivity over all else. Even if we cared about the people who worked for us, we had to meet the demands of shareholders who expected higher returns every quarter.

We never imagined that all of those former employees would figure out how to use those same tools to compete directly with us. By the mid-twenties, the entrepreneurial explosion that so many pundits had been writing about for decades finally occurred. The great irony of the gig economy was that instead of making employees obsolete, it made us, the owners, the endangered species.

This shift was brought about by the very businesses that created the so-called Uber economy. Companies like Amazon, Uber, and Airbnb replaced traditional middlemen with software. They were neither producers or even distributors in the classic sense, but a new class of digital intermediaries.

At first, they seemed cool and hip. That helped to mask the fact that they were inserting themselves into the transaction process while building the case for direct peer-to-peer exchanges. As the digital giants continued to grow, that early veneer of coolness began to wear thin.

Before long, a few folks started to wonder aloud: *If the purpose of being connected is to eliminate the middleman, why are my transactions still being managed by a corporate entity?*

Of course, we supported their drive to become monopolies. We argued that without the market gatekeepers, the whole system would collapse into chaos. We relied on the past half century of consumer trust, bought and paid for by billions in advertising to slow down the rush to completely eliminate all middlemen.

But even the best of our scare tactics couldn't stop the inevitable. Like so many other disruptions, this one grew from the fringes. Online sites like Etsy had been one of the first to prove it was possible to create true peer-to-peer economies. By the late teens, sites like it were curating billions of dollars of transactions directly between artisans and consumers. Their success rippled through the consumer marketplace. We watched helplessly as peer-to-peer platforms transformed our shiny new Uber economy into a Nuber—no one in the middle—economy. There were plenty of missteps and failures, but once the ball got rolling, we all soon found ourselves competing with millions of individual creators, sellers, and marketers.

At the same time, the growing gig economy combined with the accelerated pace of technological change to upend the traditional model of higher education. By the end of the twentieth century, education, typically a college degree, was the most valuable asset a worker could possess. Getting that degree was expensive, in both time and money. As a result, most people entered the workforce hoping that the skills they acquired in two, four, or six years, would serve them for forty or more years.

As constant and rapid change became the new normal, the single shot education model began to break down. Knowledge, whether it was technical or professional, went out of date at an alarming rate. It became apparent that granting degrees for time spent in the seat had to be replaced by dynamic and lifelong learning. At first, those of us saddled with permanent workforces had no choice but to invest heavily in continuing education for our workers. For a while, traditional colleges and universities were able to profit quite handsomely as they became little more than professional training schools conforming to the ever-shifting needs of business.

As large corporations began to shed full-time employees for gig workers, we realized it was much cheaper to simply replace outmoded workers than to retrain them. We shifted the burden of staying up to date to the independent workers.

Faced with the prospect of becoming irrelevant, universities had to react to these new demands. They began to experiment with ways to make education available to a much broader population. Digital platforms connected professors directly to learners. A new generation of educators eagerly developed methods to meet the needs of learners on their terms. We thought we had outsourced our training problems. It didn't occur to us that we were also making ourselves irrelevant. By forcing workers to take more and more responsibility for their own success we were also empowering them to chart their own futures.

Of course, we remained smugly content. We had structure and supply chains. We were the marketing behemoths. Who else had access to the manpower required to run a significant enterprise?

The employees we had cast aside began to look for new ways to thrive. They formed small loosely knit companies that had the ability to be agile and quickly adapt to new trends and technologies. Smart agents, virtual personal assistants, and even simple task management apps made it possible to offload many of the mundane tasks needed to grow a business. By the mid-twenties, digital assistants evolved into full-fledged virtual workforces. Lone entrepreneurs and short-term work collectives became the fastest growing enterprises. The future we had worked so carefully to constrain blossomed beyond our abilities to control.

In retrospect, we were complicit in our own demise.

Oh well, enough looking backward. I'll let you get back to meeting the other individuals who have been building your new tomorrows.

6

Reimagining Technology Access

Fast Sammy, the Two-Wheelin' Grocer

The delivery truck comes barreling around the corner, forcing Samuel to swerve hard toward the curve to avoid being run over. Safely out of the way, he turns and gives the truck the finger, a futile but satisfying gesture at the indignantly of having to share the road with aggressive robotrucks.

Samuel pats the frame of his bicycle like he is calming a frightened horse and looks it over for damage. "You're okay girl."

The bike is more than just his livelihood; it is his personal work of art. He spent nearly every day and night for three months at the community makerspace, designing and fabbing it. Every part, from the bright red frame to the intricately woven baskets that ride in front of the handlebars and beside each wheel; even the cargo trailer he pulls behind, is his unique design. To the casual viewer, the bike looks like it would be almost impossible to maneuver, especially if it were completely loaded. But that is the beauty of Samuel's design. He 3-D printed the bike using the latest plasteel inks. It's light enough for him to pick up with one hand but strong enough to withstand a sledgehammer or even a robotruck.

Sure that the bike is unharmed, he pauses to document the near-miss for his friend Sheila. She's running a crowd site tracing all the accidents and near accidents between autonomous vehicles and people in the community, mainly bike vendors, like Samuel.

Sheila's already collected enough data to show that the accident rate is higher in Sammy's neighborhood than it is uptown. Now she's trying to prove that the trucking companies are cutting corners on safety when they send trucks downtown. Safety protocols for autonomous vehicles are not cheap. It takes a lot of hardware and computing power to navigate crowded city streets. Turn off one of two collision avoidance sensors, dial down the required safety envelope, maybe shift to low-fi Lidar. A handful of changes on a few hundred trucks could add nicely to the owners' bottom lines.

Of course, such practices are illegal, just like other forms of discrimination have been for decades. That doesn't mean the law always get enforced. The big difference now is that citizens like Sheila have the tools necessary to expose violators. Samuel has no idea if she is right or not, but he knows that enough data will get them the answer.

He pushes hard on the pedal and guides the bike back into the street. Samuel is tall and lanky, with the muscles of a serious rider and a perpetual youthfulness. As he passes the few early morning sidewalk commuters, those who notice him would assume he is barely twenty years old. It is only when he stops at a red light that they might get a closer look and realize that the slight greying of his temples and deep creases that line his face belong to someone at least a decade older.

Soon the sun will rise above the low, ragged skyline, and grey buildings will be transformed into a vibrant technicolor backdrop. The streets will fill with people, traffic, and the cacophony of life in the city. For now, Samuel enjoys the rare quiet and solitude. It's a ten-minute ride to the re-dis center. Because of the incident, he'll be the last one to arrive, but he's not worried.

When he arrives at the heavily secured entrance, he doesn't need to stop, only slow down enough for the cameras to recognize his face. He knows exactly how fast he can pass by for the cameras to register him. He should, since he has done this so many times before. Two thousand, one hundred, twenty-three times over the past six years, three months, and two weeks to be precise. Being precise with numbers is the key to Samuel's success.

He parks his bike in front of a nondescript warehouse, one in a long row of commercial buildings at least a hundred years old. Most of the others have been transformed into small shops and businesses with bright facades that welcome the many local customers that stream by during the day. The owners of this warehouse have wasted no effort on improving the exterior. Samuel counts forty-seven bikes already parked by the warehouse entrance. He knows the owners of nearly every one of them. All of them know him. They should. He started this business.

Entering the warehouse is like stepping into another world completely. The floors and walls are gleaming white. Small warehouse bots scurry around under the watchful eye of a large robocrane. Samuel can't help but think that this is techno overkill for a place whose sole purpose is to pass off surplus produce from the Amazon/Whole Foods Go stores uptown to the mobile grocers downtown. He realizes that the look is all corporate ego. The company is more than willing to get the cred for being socially responsible and make a nice profit off merchandise they used to dump, but they still do not consider themselves part of Samuel's neighborhood.

This morning, like every morning, the space is filled with crates of produce. To the uninformed eye, there wouldn't be much to distinguish the contents from any on display at those fancy uptown stores. You might see a few more bruises here, and some of the leafy greens might have a single outer leaf on the verge of turning brown, but these are the rejects, deemed second rate and offered here without warranty or promise as the text scrolling across Samuel's augmented lenses warns in bright red letters.

Samuel certainly doesn't need the reminder of the terms and conditions for the auction. He has the eye of an expert, supplemented by the power of data. He ignores the text scrolling in front of him and heads for the first row of crates.

As he strides quickly down the aisles, sensors inside the crates relay intricate details about the contents: quantity, date harvested, hours spent in transit, even up to the moment nutritional values. The Wi-Fi in his lenses picks up the data and displays them over the actual scene. He stops now and then to give the contents of a crate a closer inspection. It's an old habit, not really necessary; Samuel possesses a keen instinct for matching just the right product to his customers. As he passes those lots that look worthwhile, he whispers the price he's willing to pay. Immediately, his bid appears on the lenses along with the bids from all the other buyers exploring the warehouse.

Samuel walks fast and covers the entire warehouse in less than twenty minutes. As he heads back to the front, he watches the developing auction. So far, so good. Few of the other buyers are competing with him on the lots he has selected. They know that Samuel has an uncanny sense for knowing exactly the right price to pay so he can still sell to his customers and make a profit.

The one exception seems to be lot number 2791. He pauses for a moment to remember which one it is. Oh yeah, a bundle of jute mallow. The leafy green, native to Africa, has been getting some notice lately in the Uptown culinary circles but is still rare; its slimy texture when cooked, off-putting to those unfamiliar with it. Samuel knows it from his Big Mama's kitchen. She grew some in a small patch outside her back door, from seeds that their ancestors had brought to this country nearly a century before.

He's spent many a Sunday afternoon there with his aunties and uncles and tons of cousins. The aunties were always whispering about Big Mama's radical lifestyle. They said she had hung out with a group of civil rights activists called the *Black Panthers* when she was young. Family lore had it that his great-grandfather might have been one of the more famous members of that group. All Big Mama would ever say about him was that he was tall, handsome, and a real go-getter, just like the young Samuel. Some of Samuel's best memories from those days were of incredible meals Big Mama and his aunties served up.

He suspects that some of his customers might have their own family memories about the jute mallow and be willing to pay a little extra. Derek, one of the younger buyers, seems to have the same idea. He's bid more than Samuel. Samuel sees Derek standing across the warehouse, trying to look nonchalant, hoping to hide his nervousness over competing with the big man. Samuel smiles and raises his bid half a cent a pound. Without hesitating, Derek responds with another half-cent raise.

Brash, Samuel thinks, *boy got some moxie.* A lot like him when he started out. He knows he should probably let it go, give it to the kid. Not much margin at this price. He's just about to turn away when his competitive streak takes over.

"Nay, you can wait a little longer before you get the better of me," he whispers. "Lot 2791, twenty-seven per." The number appears instantly.

With a shrug and a nod, Derek acknowledges that he has lost this round. Samuel returns the gesture and hopes the young man hasn't just goaded him into a bad business decision. The profit margins for a two-wheelin' grocer are razor thin. Samuel is successful because he can interpret the data and make decisions quickly. Still, he knows, better than any of the others, the risks. He should, since he practically invented the market.

Growing up in the neighborhood, Samuel had learned early on that you had to hustle to survive. Still, he never imagined that one day he would become an entrepreneur and a leader in the revitalization of his urban community.

He was only nine when he started hanging out at the corner bodega, offering to carry groceries home for the G-mommas. They'd tip him a few coins. The money was great, but Samuel was even more interested in learning why each one tipped what she did. He started trying to guess how much he was going to get. It didn't take him long to get good at it. He made a game out of it. If he guessed wrong, he'd give the whole tip to one of the vets on the corner. After that, he didn't get it wrong very often. He still dropped a little change in their cups. His Big Mama had taught him to care for his brothers.

Before long, he had earned the G-mommas' trust. They started sending him to the store to do their shopping for them. More than once, in the beginning, he got sent back because he brought them a sad-looking head of lettuce or a melon "softer than a baby's head." It was under their watchful eye that he learned how to select the best produce, even when the selection was limited to the corner bodega.

By the time he was sixteen, it was easy to get hired as a stocker at the new Amazon/Whole Foods Go Emporium uptown. During the interview, his new boss was amazed by the lanky boy's grocery knowledge.

The A/W was a long bike ride and a universe away from his neighborhood. The store was a high-tech playground filled with every imaginable distraction. Samuel had been brought up to consider carefully every choice when shopping and wasn't impressed by the store's extravagances. He understood that it was all part of the experience these uptown customers were shopping for. It certainly helped justify the ridiculous mark-ups. To be fair, they could afford to pay the prices, and the store was serious about quality and freshness—so serious that they had outfitted the store with the most advanced sensors and data grabbers.

Every individual piece of produce was monitored like a newborn in an intensive care ward. At the first sign that any was past its peak moment, Samuel would appear. His job was to make sure that the stock was constantly rotated so that no customer would ever confront a piece of produce that wasn't photoshoot worthy. He spent his days moving stock from the back of the store to the displays and moving outdated stock back to the warehouse.

He was also in charge of disposing of the unsold stock. Even without all the advanced real-time data, Samuel could have told them that they were throwing away a massive amount of good food. Sure, about half of it went to the local food charities, but by the time those items made it through a second bureaucratic distribution system, even more would be lost to waste and spoilage.

Samuel had a hard time accepting all that waste. He knew there would be a market downtown for the food that the store was tossing. The problem was distribution. But he had an idea how to solve that.

The city was full of bike delivery services. Bikers could get you food from your favorite takeout joint, scripts from the drugstore, a bottle from the neighborhood liquor store. There were even a few grocery services that delivered by bike. Samuel and all his friends picked up a few bucks now and then doing delivery. If he could convince enough of them to work with him, they could set up an alternative grocery delivery system.

When he first tried to sell the idea to his friends, he didn't get many takers. Part of it was pride, part of it was not believing the effort would be worth the return. Samuel enlisted his friend Lenny to help solve the second problem. Lenny was a coding madman. It only took him a couple of all-nighters, fueled by a six-pack of NooTroo, to create the Grocer App.

The app sucked up all the data from around the city on the prices produce was selling for in real time. Pick any item, and it could tell you immediately the average price you could expect to get, by neighborhood, even down to a specific block. Using the app, Samuel could prove that there was profit in his idea.

Still, even the young guys he needed to buy into the idea were reluctant. Pride could be the hardest obstacle to overcome in this neighborhood. That is until the G-mommas stepped in. When they learned that he could get them fresher produce at a lower price, they became his biggest recruiters. Soon, guys he didn't even know were searching him out and asking how to get in on the gig.

Convincing the managers at A/W to test the idea was a lot easier. They figured they didn't have anything to lose—just some produce they were going to trash anyway. Once word got out about the test, two-wheelin' grocers started popping up all over the city.

In the first year, the new secondary market turned a profit for the A/W. That's when they decided to go all in and set up the re-dis center. They even offered Samuel a job as assistant manager. He passed. He preferred the close relationship with his customers over managing warehouse bots like the one following him now to his bike with his purchases from the morning's auction.

Quickly and efficiently, Samuel loads the produce, putting those items he expects to deliver first near the top. He never knows for sure, since his customers will bid on the produce in a second auction. Trying to anticipate who will place the winning bids for each item is another of Samuel's games. He's gotten pretty good at it and only occasionally has to dig deep into one of the baskets when he makes his deliveries.

Loaded down with a cornucopia of fruits and vegetables, Samuel pushes hard to get the bike going and slowly pedals out of the distribution center parking lot. The first couple of blocks is always the hardest, trying to get the dead weight of 180 pounds of product moving. Finally, he picks up speed, and the bike begins to glide along. Now, if he just gets lucky with traffic, he'll have an easy twenty-block ride to his first customer.

One of those customers is Sharesa Johnstone. Right now, fresh vegetables are the farthest thing from her mind. She's rushing around the apartment trying to get her boys, Eric and Andrew, off to the neighborhood maker center where they attend classes. She shuts the door behind them just as she gets the ping that Samuel's auction is beginning. She clicks on the list and starts scrolling through the day's offerings as she goes back to the kitchen table to finish her cup of coffee. She bids on her regular items; sweet potatoes, corn, peas. Eric likes celery, so she bids on a bunch, and she's going to try zucchini one more time. Without the two-wheelin' grocers, she'd never be able to buy nearly as much fresh produce.

She's almost finished with her bids when she sees the jute mallow and is hit with a flood of memories. Her Mamaw used to make a stew with it. Mamaw said it was full of the kind of good stuff every growing child needs. She remembers how good it tasted, a little slimy like okra, but rich and earthy. Mamaw passed away almost two years ago, and Sharesa still misses her. It might be a good way to connect the boys to their history, she thinks. Her budget is tight this week, but maybe there's enough for one more small bid. She places it, afraid that it's too low and someone else will be buying this memory.

Samuel watches the auction as he pedals. The numbers projected on his lenses stand out sharply against the blurred background of the passing roadside. As soon as he gets a bid that matches his projected price he accepts. He's not trying to hustle anybody, just go home with some creds in his pocket. It looks like he's going to have a good day, bids are quickly getting to price.

He notices that there are a handful of offers on the jute. His instinct had been right. He recognizes Ms. Johnstone's name among them. She's a few cents behind the top bidder, but she's one of Samuel's best customers, always giving him five stars on Grocerater. Lots of days she even gives him a glass of her homemade sweet tea, best in the neighborhood. Besides, her Mamaw was one of his regulars when he was carrying groceries from the bodega. He accepts her bid.

Sharesa gets the ping that she has won the bid for her entire shopping cart. Estimated delivery in less than ten minutes. That's enough time to ask her kitchen app to find a recipe for jute mallow stew. The options appear on the cooktop screen and she scrolls through them until she finds the one that reminds her most her Mamaw's recipe. She selects it and the kitchen app begins to assemble the list of ingredients she already has and the ones she will need. The app will automatically order the missing ingredients from the local bodega and they will be delivered before noon.

Sharesa is engrossed in the recipe when she gets the alert that Samuel is arriving. She heads out of the kitchen, then stops and goes back to the cupboard. She gets out a glass and pulls a pitcher of dark, rich iced tea from the refrigerator. She fills the glass and goes outside to meet her two-wheelin' grocer.

Archie's Apology

Archie here again. Sorry to keep interrupting, but for those of you who may be reading this years from now, I think it's important to provide some context. The digital renaissance didn't just happen overnight. It took forty, almost fifty years for digital technology to overtake nearly every aspect of daily life. Long before that happened, many people were speculating about what this new digital age might look like. The 1980s and '90s were a particularly ripe time for this kind of speculation, especially among a new generation of science fiction writers who invented a genre called cyberpunk. One of the best-known voices of this group was William Gibson. Most of his stories were set in a near future where advances in digital technology had become so ubiquitous that almost all of life was lived in the virtual world, at least for those with the power and money. The new technologies magnified the gap between the ultra-rich and the underprivileged. The characters in these stories were often individuals struggling to survive on the fringes of this cyberworld.

I have to admit the future he created seemed frighteningly possible. When asked how he was able to imagine such convincing visions he is reported to have said, "The future is already here; it's just not evenly distributed."

As it turned out, that statement was an apt description of the new age we were creating. Whether it was the first personal computers in the 1980s, the internet in the '90s, or even the first smartphones in 2007, the miracles of the digital age came first to those with money and privilege. By the teens, it was clear that society was separating into two classes: those who were already living in the future, and those who were waiting for the latest technology to trickle down.

As digital technology became more and more essential, it was easy to imagine how this divide between the digerati and the disenfranchised could become permanent. Then, a curious thing happened. We discovered that the most important resource of the digital age was not the shiny toys we coveted but the data those devices produced.

Oh, don't misunderstand. Those of us in the business world had known this since the very early days of the internet. We had been obsessively collecting data about online users' habits since a coder by the name of Lou Montulli invented the first web browser cookie. That was way back in the early 1990s. Over the years, people have been incredibly complacent about letting their internet providers, their cell phone services, and GPS systems collect information about their activities. Online shopping and social media opened the floodgates, and soon we were all drowning in data. By 2015, the digital economy was creating and collecting more data every year than had been created in the entire history of humanity.

That was just the tip of the iceberg. The real motherlode of data came when the tech companies began connecting not just people but all of their devices. Marketers got giddy at the prospect of being able to track every time a consumer opened their refrigerator, turned up or down the thermostat, or even how often they used the toilet. They called this the *Internet of Things*. By 2025, we had connected over 50 billion things—automobiles, buildings, home appliances. This new internet was creating billions of gigabytes of new data every day.

Those of us running the biggest corporations were enamored by the sheer size of this ever-expanding data universe. We hired the smartest data analysts and bought the fastest supercomputers to extract meaning from all these bits and bytes. We made big data into our next big business.

Once we had built that massive collection infrastructure, the incremental cost of collecting data plummeted, just as we had planned. At the same time, the power of computers we needed to analyze massive data sets continued to soar. Before long, everything from traffic on the highways to produce in the grocery stores could be tracked and analyzed.

Suddenly, almost anyone could afford access to the great data stream. The digital divide that we had been building started to crumble. Cheap data helped jumpstart the micro-entrepreneur movement. Access to precise data, focused on a local population, became a powerful tool for discovering innovative solutions to problems that had once seemed intractable, or at the very least unprofitable.

Data created a new marketplace for socially oriented businesses. Because they were able to connect with multiple supply chains, adapt to fluctuations in prices of goods and services in real time, and quantify the results of their efforts, these social entrepreneurs could turn a profit and help their local communities.

The new micro-entrepreneur class began to spring up in communities across the country. They brought renewed economic vibrancy and, more importantly, hope to communities we had written off. Most importantly, they gave those communities the power to imagine their own futures.

We were believers in the technodreams future brought to us by our friends in Silicon Valley. So much so that we failed to see the obvious flaw in their hyper-rational individualism. It lacked connection to community traditions and values and left too many people feeling like their only choice was someone else's future or their own crumbling past.

The great disruption of our digital age was to make us all realize that every future is local and unique. Empowered by the tools that make bottom-up change possible and fueled by the millennial generation's new found embrace of community and tradition, local solutions spread. To those who are creating community futures, tomorrow seems less like a giant leap into the unknown.

7

Reimagining Suburbia

Allie Chase Brings the NEWS!

The Amanpour had been zipping back and forth overhead like a mutant hawk on meth for nearly ten minutes. Despite its advanced AI, visual recognition capabilities, and audio pattern algorithms, it still had not been able to make any sense out of the cacophony taking place in the great hall. With the equivalent of a robotic sigh, the drone floated to a point just below the ceiling, set itself to record a wide shoot of the chaos below, and sent out a call for help.

Allie Chase was on duty when the ping came in a few minutes after 6:00 p.m. It was a typically slow Friday night. She was monitoring about a dozen drones capturing local news streams. Allie had gone into journalism with big dreams of traveling to exotic places and being in the middle of the action on the ground. Spending her nights sitting in a windowless office in a nondescript office park, watching newsfeeds from boring little towns she could never imagine wanting to visit, was about as far from her dream job as she could get. Still, it was a paying—and mostly mindless—gig that gave her plenty of time to develop material for her personal channel.

She glanced up at the notification floating in front of the lens of her smartglasses. The call was coming from a drone assigned to cover a community council meeting. *That was odd,* she thought. Council meetings were about as straightforward and boring as any news could possibly be. They barely met the minimum requirements to be considered stream worthy. In fact, no one actually watched the streams. They were captured for the data miners looking to collect personal data on the handful of participants who regularly showed up to complain about their neighbors or the lack of municipal services.

Occasionally, some truly weird stuff would happen at one of the meetings. They did tend to attract the local fringe elements. A concerned citizen screaming and yelling about their smart toaster sending them alien messages in the night or an amateur dance group's performance that resembled a riot could confuse even the most advanced drone. It was likely the Amanpour simply needed a minute to reassess the situation and recalibrate parameters. Since she had nothing better to do, Allie decided to take a look.

She called up the drone's stream and immediately did a double take, checking to make sure it was at the right location. The scene certainly didn't look like a council meeting. For one thing, the place was packed. There must have been close to a thousand people there. Even council meetings in the large cities rarely drew more than a couple dozen people.

Allie was intrigued. She swiped the air in front of her and the drone's controls appeared on her virtual dashboard. She leaned forward and commanded, "Manual override."

The image onscreen dipped and fluttered as the drone reacted to giving up control. It took her only a few seconds to get it steadied and then with a practiced move she sent it in a graceful arc down closer to the action. The drone buzzed silently just above the heads of the crowd. Allie tipped its single big eye down toward the action to get a better idea of what was going on.

Up close, the scene looked more like a community festival or celebration than an official meeting. People were clustered in small groups; eating, drinking, chatting. Kids were running around and playing. There were stages set up throughout the hall where actors, dancers, and even a live band, were performing. There didn't seem to be any kind of organized meeting taking place.

She was still trying to make sense of the scene when the drone's warning klaxon sounded in her ear. She looked upward in the direction of the sound and the drone's giant eye swiveled to follow her gaze. A brightly colored fish was diving straight toward her. Allie made a quick evasive maneuver as the fish screamed by, just missing her drone by inches. She steadied herself and pivoted to watch as the flying fish swooped down to join a whole pod of robotic sea creatures cavorting over the heads of laughing and giggling children.

Allie sent her drone higher to float in safer airspace. She could see now why it had been confused. This scene was way outside all the event parameters for a robotic council reporter, even an advanced one like the Amanpour. As the drone continued to stream the panoramic image of the activity below, she called up the event brief and began to read the words scrolling in front of her glasses.

FIESTAVILLE COMMUNITY COUNCIL MEETING
TAKES PLACE THE THIRD FRIDAY OF EVERY MONTH,
IN THE COMMUNITY COMMON HALL.
HOURS 5 PM – 8 PM LOCAL TIME.

Seems pretty straightforward, Allie thought, until she discovered the special note that had been added in bright red.

FIESTAVILLE IS A STAKEHOLDER-OWNED COMMUNITY WITH
A POPULATION OF APPROXIMATELY 1123.
COUNCIL MEETINGS ARE MANDATORY FOR ALL RESIDENTS
BETWEEN THE AGES OF 16–96.
EFFECTIVE STREAMING OF EVENT REQUIRES AT LEAST THREE DRONES
AND MAY NECESSITATE LIVE PILOTING.

Allie glanced up at the image coming from the drone. Well, that certainly explained what she was observing. It also sparked her reporter's instincts. She needed to know more about this community.

She quickly checked her GPS map and located the two closest standby drones. She redirected them to Fiestaville. It would take them about three minutes to arrive onsite. That gave her time to do some research on Fiestaville.

"Sherlock, tell me about Fiestaville."

She listened to the research AI's report as she monitored the two incoming drones and continued to survey the colorful scene below.

"Fiestaville, aka Fiesta Mall, aka Fiesta Bay Entertainment Complex, was originally constructed in 1977. The mall contains over 1.36 million square feet of enclosed commercial space situated on approximately seventy acres. When it first opened, it featured four anchor tenants, a food court, movie theater, and more than 140 individual retail establishments. By the end of the first decade of the twenty-first century, the mall had suffered from the decline in onsite retail that impacted shopping malls across the country. This situation was driven by changing demographics and the rise of online shopping. The mall was sold in 2012 to the Lancaster Consortium,

who at the time was transforming suburban malls into so-called entertainment centers. One of the original anchor stores was turned into a fitness center, a second became an indoor soccer training facility, and a childcare center was opened in a third. Despite these changes, the mall continued to struggle financially, never reaching more than 50 percent capacity.

"In 2018 the consortium terminated the remaining leases and closed the mall. The structure sat empty for nearly two years until Wells Fargo Commercial Bank finalized the foreclosure and announced plans to demolish the property. Shortly after that announcement, the Fiestaville Stakeholders approached the bank with a plan to purchase the property and turn it into a cooperative residential community. The group raised nearly 50 million dollars through an Indiegogo campaign in less than four months—A record at the time for the crowdfunding platform.

"Today, Fiestaville is home to approximately 300 families. It also contains forty-five retail shops and a common area and food hall operated by the residents. The soccer center remains. The former childcare center has been repurposed as a maker lab and learning center. The movie theater has been transformed into a live and virtual performance space and hosts a highly regarded Esports tournament. During the residential renovation of the mall, the stakeholders added a 100,000-square-foot vertical farming space, 25 acres of traditional outdoor growing space, and over 20,000 solar panels.

"Fiestaville is just one of many former shopping malls to be repurposed as professional, educational, or residential space. Of the more than 1,100 shopping malls in America in 2005, fewer than 300 were still operating as retail spaces in 2030.

"Fiestaville is unique in its governing structure. It was granted

township status and operates as a completely independent entity. It has no elected officials, but a board of town managers chosen by lottery serve as administrators. All town policies are decided by a public vote of residents. All residents over the age of sixteen are required to participate in all public votes.

"In addition, . . . "

"Well damn, Sherlock," Allie muttered as she cut the research transmission. "So that's how you get everyone to show up for a council meeting. Force them."

But as she surveyed the animated crowd, it was hard to imagine that anyone there felt forced to attend. They seemed to be enjoying the experience way too much. She definitely needed to get closer to the action to understand what was going on.

The other two drones had arrived and were floating nearby. Allie quickly transmitted instructions for them to collect generic B-stream around the mall. She grabbed the virtual controls and aimed her drone down toward the crowd below.

"Search for local spokespersons."

Instantly the drone's facial recognition software projected data overlays on the sea of faces.

"Whoa major overload," Allie realized she needed to narrow the field. As she pulled the drone back up for a long shot, she muttered to herself: *Now where would I be if I were an organizer?"*

Before she even finished her thought, she spotted them. A small cluster of people standing next to the largest stage, empty except for a lone podium. As she zoomed toward them, her reporter's instincts told her that this serious-looking group had to be the meeting organizers. She was pretty sure she would find at least one of the city managers among them.

As she scanned each face in medium close-up, her hunch was

proven correct. All were current members of the council. She considered whom to approach and ask for an interview. She noticed one woman in her mid-fifties, with slightly greying hair, listening intently to one of her more animated colleagues. There was an openness about her that Allie suspected meant she would be a willing subject.

"Subject profile," Allie whispered.

"Pamela Yang, age fifty-four. Resides in unit 104 with her partner David Whitefeather. Electrical engineer, current member of the manager's council, term expires in six months. Founding stakeholder of Fiestaville."

"Score," Allie smiled.

While Allie waited for the conversation below to end, she felt the urge to check her makeup and hair; an unnecessary holdover from her days as anchor of her college TV news show. Tonight, her interview subject would be interacting with Allie's avatar, who was always perfectly coiffed and poised.

The woman finally stopped talking. Pamela took her hand, leaned in close and thanked her for her suggestions. She promised to follow up and get back to her as soon as possible. Satisfied, the younger woman turned and walked away.

Seeing her chance, Allie activated her sub-vocal message channel. "Excuse me, Ms. Yang. Allie Chase of Buzzfeed local news streaming service here. We're livestreaming your community meeting, and I was wondering if I could grab a few comments from you?"

Pamela looked up and saw the drone hovering overhead. She smiled, nodded yes and indicated that they should step away from the crowd. The Amanpour followed as she led the way to a quieter corner where there was a table and empty chair.

She turned back to the drone; "Mind if I sit?"

"Please make yourself comfortable," Allie replied.

Pamela sat and looked straight at the drone hovering just three feet in front of her. To a casual observer, it looked as if the woman and the machine with the one bug eye were engaged in a staring contest. What Pamela saw was the slightly ethereal image of Allie's face floating in front of her.

"Ms. Yang, thank you for taking the time to talk with me. I have to start out by saying that this is not your normal town council meeting."

Pamela laughed. " 'Normal' is not a word we use to describe much of anything about Fiestaville. You know, we're one of the first stakeholder towns. Please call me Pamela."

"Well, Pamela, tell me a little bit about how this all came about. You're one of the original stakeholders, correct?"

"Reluctant founder is a better description. David, my partner, heard about the idea first. When he told me he thought we should leave the city to live in the suburbs, in an abandoned shopping mall, no less; well, let's just say my first reaction was less than enthusiastic."

"What made you change your mind?"

"As much as I loved living in the city, life was getting stressful. The local government couldn't keep up with the pressures of rapid growth; infrastructure was crumbling, the price of everything kept going up."

"Those problems are pretty widespread in the larger cities," Allie observed.

"True. Like most people, I had bought into the myth that I had to accept all the inconveniences for the advantages that living in a vibrant, exciting city offered. My image of the suburbs was pretty bleak. I remembered them from my youth as being sterile and boring. More recently the news streams had portrayed them as abandoned and even dangerous.

"I let Dave drag me to a couple of meetings and I realized that suburban pioneers were a really interesting group of people. They had all these crazy dreams, but there was something about the way they talked that made it easy to believe they could make their dreams come true. We imagined a community that had a sense of togetherness without sacrificing innovation and diversity."

"Like governing by direct participation? That's a pretty radical idea. How's that working for you?" Allie asked, unable to mask her skepticism.

Pamela laughed loudly. "Yeah crazy idea, right? Honestly, sometimes it can be a pain, but we manage to muddle through. So far, we've been able to keep the lights on and even deal with a handful of pretty contentious issues. Keeping the community informed and actively engaged is a critical part of making it work. I'm not going to lie; it takes work. In the end, I think it makes us better neighbors."

"But you require participation, like this meeting tonight. How do enforce something like that?"

"Oh, we have our methods." Pamela responded with a grin. "Seriously, it's not so hard. Most people are willing to pitch in as long as the system is well organized. We make sure that the monthly meetings are a celebration of the community. Most people see them as a chance to get together with neighbors and friends. We always make sure there are plenty of distractions for the children. Most of the real work happens before the meeting, in the cloud. Anyone can bring up an issue and most issues get resolved there. Usually, we only have one of two major issues to vote on at the actual meeting.

"One of the biggest fallacies that people believe is that local decision-making is difficult or requires special skills. At this level, most of the issues are straightforward and require good old common sense."

Before Allie could get out her next question, every com device in the place chimed, followed by an announcement that, amplified a thousand times, filled the hall.

"Please come to order for the monthly meeting of the Fiestaville Town Council."

Allie noticed that a young man around her age was now standing at the podium onstage.

"Fiestaville, are you ready to govern?!" He called out like an announcer at a sporting event.

The response was deafening. The crowd's cheers rang off the hard walls and ceiling.

"Awesome! Before we start, I just want to remind everyone to check our great food vendors. They've gone totally mega for us tonight. I am told Dave has a new burger recipe that some claim tastes just like hamburger, whatever that means. And rumor has it that Lynn is tapping one of her special kegs this evening. So, plenty of choices for everyone."

Allie was impressed. The young man certainly looked at ease whipping up the crowd.

He continued. "There were five proposals up for vote this month. Looks like about 75 percent of you have already voted. Thank you for your participation. Now for you slackers out there, I have one word for you: Payola."

He had to pause for the cheers and applause from the crowd.

"It's been another record-breaking month for profits. I know you want your share, so let's get off the stick, okay?

He was interrupted again by more applause and cheering. Allie thought that the meeting seemed more like an old-fashioned revival than any community meeting she had ever covered.

"I'm gonna give you a couple of minutes right now to get 'er done before we start tonight's Main Event."

The band began to play as the young man stepped away from the podium. Allie turned to Pamela.

"You pay people to vote?"

"We distribute a monthly allowance to all stakeholders of voting age in the community. The only requirement is that they vote and attend council meetings."

"So, you do bribe people to participate. I knew this was too good to be true."

Pamela smiled that easy smile again. She had answered these same questions many times before.

"We consider it positive reinforcement. The money is theirs anyway. The co-op owns the solar panel fields and the greenhouses. Both produce substantially more than we can use. We sell the surplus to the surrounding communities. All stakeholders get an equal share of the profits."

"And you're able to manage all that without a full-time city government?" Allie asked.

"Blockchain has made it possible to automate most of the processes. Plus, the twelve members of the city management council have to be available at least eight hours a week for community matters. You'd be surprised how many residents are willing to volunteer when we ask them."

Allie paused trying to take it all in. She was feeling a little overloaded.

"One last question. Do you think this experiment is scalable?

"That's a good one. We're about to find out." Pamela replied.

Before Allie could ask her what she meant, the young man returned to the podium.

"Alright! Alright! There are still seventy-seven, no wait, make that seventy-one, of you who have not cast your ballots, and yes, I know where you live. Hey, no prob, if you don't want your share this month, just let me know and I'll be glad to vote for you."

"Now it's time for tonight's maaain eeevent."

Without missing a beat, the young man shed the announcer persona and turned serious.

"Tonight, we have before us a very important and serious topic. The question is: should Fiestaville grant citizenship to the refugees we have been hosting in temporary shelters?"

As he continued, images of the refugee camp appeared on large screens floating throughout the hall. Seen from the point of view of a drone, the camp was made up of more than a hundred small, domed structures that looked like plastic igloos. They occupied a small corner of the mall's once-massive parking lot.

"The camp was established eighteen months ago when you voted, almost unanimously, to host families whose homes had been destroyed in the worst floods this region has ever seen. Since that time, we have taken in more than 120 families and the total population of the camp is now 325. That number includes seven children born in the camp.

"This proposal was introduced at last month's meeting, I know all of you have had time to give it due consideration. It's been the topic of quite a few discussions, some of them admittedly heated. Let's be honest; this is an important decision. Whatever you decide tonight will shape the future of our community. As is our tradition, we will hear from one representative for and one against the proposal before we take a vote. I know you all will give them your attention and respect. First up, in support of the proposition, is Ms. Leslie Furness."

A tall, lean woman in her late sixties vaulted up the steps to the stage and crossed to the podium to applause from the audience. She hugged the MC and turned to address the crowd.

"Many of you know me. I was one of the founding stakeholders, and I want to urge you with all my heart to support this significant proposition. When we first set out to build this community, everybody told us it was impossible. They said we wouldn't be able to raise the money. But we did, in record time. No way would the state and county grant us a township they said. We were one of the first independent micro-townships in the state. And of course, they told us we wouldn't be able to make it last. Well, we've been here for nearly ten years now, and we're considered a model for the future of direct participatory local government. And I don't know anybody here who doesn't think this is the best place in the world to live!"

The audience erupted into cheers and applause.

She motioned for them to quiet down. "Please, I only have a couple of minutes."

The crowd quickly obeyed and she continued. "We have succeeded not because of any one person or even one small group of people. We are here because all of us have worked toward the same dream. We came here in search of new beginnings. Just like pioneers throughout history, you are the brave and slightly crazy ones willing to risk the known for a dream of a better life. That passion, that commitment, is what makes Fiestaville special.

"I've had the good fortune to get to know and work with many of the folks living in the camp. They have volunteered their time and effort to help make our community better. They all want the same thing that brought each of you here—a chance for a better tomorrow.

"Some have argued that we can't afford to invite these people to become stakeholders. They say that the extra burden will threaten the stability of our community. Those are the voices of fear, and we must never give in to them. If we had listened to the naysayers in the beginning, this community would have remained nothing but a dream. But we turned that dream into a reality, and now I say we have an important decision to make about keeping that original dream alive. Vote yes with me on this proposal. Thank you."

Allie was surprised by the intensity of the crowd's response. Many people stood to applaud and cheer. As the speaker left the stage, she passed by another young man about Allie's age. From the look on his face, she guessed he was the speaker against the proposition. As he watched the crowd, it was clear that he wasn't looking forward to his time at the podium. What happened next totally surprised Allie. Leslie stopped when she reached the young man and gave him a long hug and patted him on the shoulder as if to say it was going to be alright.

The crowd finally settled down and the MC moved back toward the podium. As Allie settled in to listen to the next speech, she realized she had never imagined that governing could be so exciting, dramatic, and yes, even fun. Maybe it was time for her to visit at least one of those boring towns she had been watching from afar.

Archie's Apology

There was a time when you couldn't go wrong investing in real estate. Shopping malls were the best. Oh, we didn't own them; that was a sucker's game. No, the real money was in development. Put up 20 percent or less of the construction costs, and the banks and the developers took all the risk. In return, you got all your profits out before the place even opened. It was like printing money.

It was no surprise that the country went on a retail building spree: mega-malls, entertainment complexes, strip malls. For a time, it looked like we would turn every open space in the suburbs into a piece of retail paradise.

I wasn't particularly surprised when the crash came. The market was severely overbuilt even before the online boom threatened brick and mortar retail. When the malls started to empty out, those of us with the money to invest concluded that the era of the suburbs was over.

Not much future when your mall becomes little more than a hangout for opioid addicts, truants, and the homeless looking to stay warm. It was time to move on, and we did, without a second thought about the wreckage we left behind. It turns out that where we saw only abandoned decaying buildings, others were able to imagine building a vibrant new future.

As a generation found themselves crowded out of the urban boom, many started looking for new frontiers. They saw opportunities in the neighborhoods where their parents had grown up and then left behind.

The new suburban pioneers were determined not to repeat the mistakes we had made. They could have easily sprawled across the open wasteland of abandoned McMansions in once exclusive gated communities. Instead, they built villages inside derelict shopping malls, schools, and office complexes. When we dismissed their efforts as doomed to fail, they responded by proving their independence. They pioneered a new wave of renewable micro-grids, closed-loop waste systems, and resource conservation.

These small, self-sufficient communities were springing up at the same time that the traditional local governments were dwindling away. We had depleted their tax base and refused to fund their crumbling infrastructure, effectively reducing them to ghost institutions. City and county governments that had never imagined that their authority would be challenged, had no choice but to sit idly on the sidelines and watch as these new settlers experimented with radical ideas about local government. They set-up direct democracies, co-ops, and collectives. Some even offered new settlers a guaranteed basic income. Others employed tools, like Blockchain, to ensure authentic and transparent representation for all.

The age of the malls had been driven by our mad desire to scale. Every project had to be bigger, better, and offer more than the one before. We were, I am afraid, obsessed with building temples to our own greatness.

In this new digital age, you measure power by the breadth of your social reach, not the spread of your physical footprint. Ideas are the most valuable products. The best ones, no matter where they are born, become currency across the networks of our connected culture. The communities they built have demonstrated that it is possible to scale in ways that are positive and sustainable. That came as a real shock to those of us who believed that the only road to profit was to sprawl across the landscape.

8

Reimagining Rural Life

Vedja Goes on a Date, Sorta

"He's here," Monica calls out. She's perched on the arm of the second-hand sofa in front of the big picture window of the old farm house. Faded bedsheets that serve as make-shift curtains for the window hide her from the outside.

"What's he driving, what's he driving?" Victoria demands, drying her hands on a tattered dishtowel as she enters the living room from the kitchen.

"A beat-up old pickup. Looks like a corn burner."

"Knew he would be. What about the hat? He's got the hat, right?" Victoria crosses the sparsely furnished living room and joins Monica by the window. Side by side, the two women are a study in contrast. Both are in their late twenties but they look like they come from completely different universes.

Monica is tall and muscular. Her long blonde hair is pulled back in a ponytail and hidden under a cap with a faded SmartAg logo.

Her strong hands are calloused from physical labor. Her fingernails are broken and chipped. She looks perfectly in place in this slightly ramshackle old farmhouse.

Victoria, on the other hand, looks like she belongs in some hipster hangout in a big city. Her hair color might be blonde, brunette, red, or even purple. All four colors and a handful of others seem to shimmer from her locks enhanced by the latest nanotech treatments. The same is true for her perfectly manicured, iridescent nails. Her outfit is more sedate but still stylish. A pair of bamboo fiber cargo shorts and a preppy madras shirt somehow work together, revealing a woman who takes time to plan her look even when she's not leaving the house.

They two women peer out the window together. A tall, lanky young man wearing jeans, a western shirt, boots, and a black cowboy hat, gets out of the pickup truck parked in front of the house.

"Black, Stetson. Nailed it. Do I know my cowboys or what?" Victoria laughs and pumps her arm in the air.

"Vee, he's kinda cute." Monica turns from the window and addresses the third woman in the room. She is sitting on the couch, her face partially hidden by a pair of mixed reality glasses. Like the other two, she is in her late twenties. She wears work dungarees, and an old faded T-shirt with the words Too Busy Farming for Ur Drama across the front.

"He's rocking those tight jeans for sure," Victoria coos.

Vee removes the glasses. "If either one of you wants to take my place, feel free," she says. "I have plenty of work to do on these plans for the new greenhouse."

"Oh no, he's here for you, Girl," Victoria replies.

"Lucky me," Vee mutters.

"Well if you weren't so damned beautiful, then the boys wouldn't be falling all over you everywhere we go," Monica adds. "Just like college. All the guys fall for Vee; we're just her poor pitiful friends. It's like Cinderella and her stepsisters."

Vee considers her two housemates and business partners. Neither looks like a forlorn stepsister. She would be quick to say they are way more attractive than her. Vee has always felt self-conscious about her round face, dark skin, and long black hair. Since moving to this isolated farming community with Monica and Victoria, that feeling of otherness has been magnified. She's continually surprised that people still think it's okay to start a conversation by asking where she's from. In fact, she is second-generation Indian-American. Her grandparents moved to this country from Mumbai when they were both teenagers. Vee grew up in a very typical midwestern suburb.

The young cowboy knocks on the door. Monica and Victoria both rush to open it. Monica reaches it first. She flings it open as Victoria is still sliding to a stop. She barely avoids crashing into their visitor as both women sing out, "Hello."

Startled, the cowboy takes a step back. Once he's sure no one is going to tackle him, he cautiously leans toward the door. "Uh, hi. I'm Buck. Here to pick up Vee."

Victoria steps back and yells dramatically. "Vedja, your date's here."

Vee gives them a scowl as she tosses her glasses on a dining room table covered in electronic equipment. She crosses to the front door.

She greets Buck with a simple, "Hey."

All of them stand there silently. Monica and Victoria's goofy smiles reveal how much they are enjoying the awkwardness of the moment.

Buck finally summons the courage to speak, "Uh, so you ready to go . . . to the rodeo." Before Vee has a chance to answer, Victoria steps in. "Girl, you are *not* going to your first rodeo dressed like that. People around here take their rodeos seriously. You gotta look your best, not like you're getting ready to work the fields. Am I right, cowboy?

"Uh, yeah, I guess. I mean, you look fine." Embarrassed, he looks down at the floor. Noticing Vee's bare feet, he offers; "You might want to put on some shoes, you know we're going to be around livestock and all."

Victoria pushes Vee toward the stairs. "You can wear those new boots in my closet. And put on a decent pair of shorts. Remember, girl, you represent the Triple V now."

Vee clomps up the stairs, leaving Buck at the mercy of the other two.

"Well don't just stand there, come on in," Monica says, as she steps back from the doorway.

Buck wipes his feet carefully and takes off his hat before stepping inside.

"I'm Monica, and this is Victoria." Monica offers her hand.

Buck returns the gesture and they shake hands. He turns to shake hands with Victoria, but she offers him a fist bump instead. Somewhat confused he closes his hand and taps knuckles with her. She grins at him as he tries not to stare at her color-shifting hair.

"Uh, nice to meet you both."

"You from around here, Buck?" Victoria asks.

"Grew up just down the road. In fact, I worked this spread a couple of summers, back when the Murphy's were still living here, running cattle and sheep."

Victoria steps closer and gives him a thorough once-over. "So, you *are* a real cowboy?"

Buck takes a step backwards to escape Victoria's intrusion into his space. "I grew up on a ranch. Like most everybody else around here. We had about 150 acres.

Victoria keeps after him. Stepping closer again, she goes full detective mode on him. "Your family still running that ranch?"

This time Buck doesn't retreat. In fact, he leans in towards her and responds with a hint of defiance, "No, my folks had to sell out about ten years ago, just couldn't make it work anymore. They tried, that's for sure."

Monica senses that the conversation is going to a place that's uncomfortable so she chimes in. "That sucks," she says softly. "I hear it's been tough for a lotta folks around here the last twenty years."

"Life has certainly changed around here. Hardly anybody trying to ranch anymore," Buck says wistfully. There's an awkward pause.

Monica reaches out and touches him gently on the arm. "C'mon in, have a seat. No telling how long Vee's gonna be."

Buck looks around the room. There aren't a lot of options. It's the old sofa or a couple of straight-backed chairs by what was once a dining room table that has been turned into work desk. He goes for the sofa.

Concerned that the old sagging sofa might swallow him up, he carefully places himself on the front edge of the cushion. Monica sits at the other end while Victoria goes to get one of the dining room chairs.

As she carries the chair across the room she calls out toward the stairs. "Vee! Better hurry up, Girl—I think we're making your date nervous." She plops the chair down, back facing the sofa, and sits on it backwards, arms draped over the chair's back.

Monica looks at Buck and shakes her head. "Ignore her. She's our marketing guru, all drama. So, are your folks still in the area?"

Buck realizes he's still clutching his hat tightly. He forces himself to relax and lays the hat down next to him. "Actually, they got to keep the house and about ten acres. They raise a few horses now. I help out when I can, but these days I work for the county, water management."

"That's got be a tough job with the droughts," Monica observes.

"Just another reason for people to give up and move away." Buck shifts uneasily on the sofa. "Not many people see much future in working the land around here." He looks down at his boots.

Victoria tips her chair forward until she almost falls over. "Well, we're definitely gonna see what we can do about that."

The chair slams back down. Monica and Buck both jump.

"So, why the heck did you guys move to this backwater?" He scans the sparse collection of mismatched furnishings in the room. A few of the items were obviously abandoned by the previous owners. The rest look like they were randomly picked up at the local thrift. "If you don't mind me asking," Buck adds quickly.

"We get that question a lot," Monica replies. "It seems folks around here still find it hard to imagine that three young women want to run their own ranch."

"Whoa now, I didn't realize you were planning on running stock. I gotta say, that seems like a pretty foolish idea." Buck shakes his head in disbelief. "You do realize that most of the big ranches have gone outta business, what with the cost of feed, water, and the fact that veggie meat is flooding the market."

"Our herd's a little different," Victoria interjects, with a mischievous smile.

Before Buck can ask what she means, Vee comes down the stairs, wearing cut-off shorts, a fancy western shirt with pearl buttons, and a pair of black and pink boots.

Buck immediately stands up and fumbles for his hat.

Victoria lets out a low whistle. "Damn Girl! Now you look ready for some ropin' and ridin'. Don't you think so, cowboy?"

Before Buck has to figure out how to respond to that leading question, Vee saves him. "I'm sure you've had enough of these two. C'mon, let's get you outta here." She crosses and takes Buck by the arm.

Victoria jumps up from her chair and calls out, "You two have fun now."

They are just past the threshold when their escape is momentarily interrupted by the sound of an alarm coming from the dining table. Both turn to see what is going on. Monica jumps up from the sofa and crosses to the table. She digs through the pile of miscellaneous papers and equipment until she recovers the tablet with an alarm flashing on its screen. She looks down at it and her eyes go wide.

"It's the filtration system."

"Crap," Vee mutters. She starts toward Monica.

Victoria cuts her off. "Relax—we got this, right Mon? You go have fun."

Monica considers the text on the tablet. "Yeah, It's probably just a faulty sensor."

Victoria turns Vee around and gives her a little push back toward Buck. She looks past to the cowboy. "She thinks just because she has a PhD in information systems she's the only one around her who can reset a sensor. You two go, have—" Before she can finish, the alarm sounds a second time.

This time Vee doesn't hesitate. She runs past the other two women and through the kitchen. The sound of the backdoor slamming jerks the others out of their momentary freeze.

Victoria looks at Buck. "Well cowboy, how'd you like to see our barn?"

All three follow Vee to the barn behind the house. When they arrive, the door is open. Vee has already disappeared inside. As Buck follows the other two in, he is immediately hit by hot moist air, a humidity foreign to these high, dry plains. It takes him a second to catch his breath in the dampness. Then he notices the smell, not a bad odor, but unlike anything he's ever smelled inside a barn. It's sweet, but with a tang of ammonia that makes his eyes water.

He blinks and looks around the barn. Twenty large round, green tanks fill the space. Each one must be at least twelve feet in diameter and four feet tall. He takes a step closer to the first tank and peers inside. It is filled with fast moving silver flashes. At first, he's not sure what he's watching.

"What the heck are you raising in here?" Then it dawns on him. "You're fish farmers?"

"Barramundi ranchers," Victoria informs him before leaving to join Vee, who is already standing in front of a control panel on the wall.

Buck is fascinated by the movement in the tank. The fish are about a foot long and look a little like the bass he caught with his dad when he was a kid. The ones in this tank seem agitated, almost angry.

All three women are huddled in front of a control panel on the wall.

Vee assesses the situation first. "Looks like the filters in tanks 3, 7, and 16 all failed."

"Those are the full-growns. We're supposed to harvest next week," Monica's adds, a sense of growing urgency in her typically calm voice.

"Ammonia's already spiked in all three tanks. Don't know how the system missed the shut-down for so long. If we don't move them now we'll lose the whole herd," Vee replies and looks over her shoulder toward the tanks.

"Move them where?" Victoria asks. "All the other tanks are full!"

"We'll have to herd them back into the juvie tanks." Vee heads for the tanks.

"They'll eat the babies!" Victoria cries out after her.

Monica grabs Victoria by the arm. "Better than losing our first harvest. C'mon. Grab some nets."

Vee is working furiously to open the hatch connecting the tank to the fish spillway. Buck, still not quite sure what is going on, joins her.

"How can I help?" he asks.

She continues to work on the cover. "We need to get these fish into this spillway and to the next tank over. Only problem is the system is designed to flow the other way. We have to get them to swim upstream."

"How do you do that?"

"We need to figure out a way to herd them." Vee gets the last fastener out of the cover and drops it to the floor.

Buck thinks for a minute and then climbs into the tank.

Vee stops and stares at him. "What the . . . "

Buck tries to corner one of the fish but quickly discovers that a cowboy is no match for a fish in water.

"You'll never catch them, just try to move them toward the opening," Vee instructs.

Buck looks around for something to help him. Seeing nothing within reach, he takes off his hat and dunks it underwater. He tries to use it as a paddle to push the fish toward the opening. His first attempt fails. He squats down deeper, with only his head above water and tries again. The first of the barramundi slides into the spillway, trying to escape.

"You got one!" Vee screams, just as Monica and Victoria arrive with long-handled nets for all.

Monica hands one to Buck. "I like your style, cowboy, but this might be a little easier. Welcome to your first fish round-up".

Vee grabs another net and starts to climb into the tank. Victoria stops her.

"Whoa there, girl. Those boots cost $400.00."

Vee kicks off the boots and climbs over the edge. She positions herself on the opposite side of Buck, and they begin to maneuver the fish toward the spillway. Monica starts working to open the second tank's spillway hatch.

Victoria joins her. She looks over at Vee and Buck and says, "As much fun as diving into a tank full of fish crap looks, I think we can probably do this better from out here."

Monica agrees. Using the nets, they circle the tank and begin to herd the fish toward the spillway.

Even with the nets, it takes nearly half an hour to finish the first two tanks. With all four working together on the third tank, they manage to finish in half the time. When the last fish is safe, they gather around a crowded tank.

The scene in the water is one of silvery chaos. The larger fish, already agitated by the move, go crazy when they realize they are surrounded by tasty morsels. Fins fly as they devour the baby fish. Victoria is the first to step away.

"I can't watch this."

The others follow her toward the door.

"At least we saved the harvest," Vee offers.

Monica nods her head in agreement. "Not much else we can do

now. I'll order replacement parts for the filter systems. Should have the tanks back up in a couple of days. Then we'll have to clean up and start over."

"Right now, we need to get you two in some dry clothes," Monica looks Buck up and down. "Not sure what we have for you to borrow."

"No problem," he laughs. "I've got some work clothes in the truck."

Later, after everyone has cleaned up, Buck, Vee, and Monica are sitting on three ancient metal yard chairs lined up across the back porch. For the first time, Buck has a chance to get a good look at the grounds around the house. Beyond the barn is a new state of the art greenhouse. Further out, in what used to be the pasture, a half-dozen windmills turn slowly in the summer breeze, surrounded by rows of neatly planted switchgrass.

"That's a pretty fancy greenhouse," he says. "I assume you're running a closed loop system?"

Monica answers, "Yep, wastewater from the fish tanks irrigates and feeds the vegetables. The plants filter out the yucky stuff, and then we re-circulate it into the fish tanks."

Buck whistles, "Must have cost you a lot to set this all up."

Monica smiles, happy to be talking about her passion, the nitty gritty of operating the farm. "Sweat equity, mainly. We pretty much spent all we had just buying the place. We convinced our college professors to lend us a bunch of students to help us build the greenhouse. That was a crazy time." She chuckles at the memory.

"Most of the greenhouse was 3-D printed onsite," Vee adds.

Buck gets up and walks to the edge of the porch. He leans over the rail and looks out at the fields. "Looks like your pasture's been taken over by weeds. You got plans for it?"

Monica stands up and joins him. She looks out over the fields. "Switchgrass. That's actually our first cash crop. We got a grant from the international carbon sequestration fund to plant it. Pretty much grows itself and sucks up carbon from the atmosphere. The utility company paid for the windmill installs, in exchange for providing our excess power to them."

Vee laughs. Buck turns back toward her as she explains. "So far the only thing we've harvested is wind. But thanks to you we'll have our first fish harvest," she smiles at Buck.

Buck shuffles in place, unsure how to respond, his face turning red. He is saved by Victoria coming out of the kitchen, carrying a tray with four glasses filled with a dark amber liquid. She puts the tray on the table and picks up a glass.

She hands the glass to Buck and explains, "Cider made from the heirloom apples, grown right here on the property."

Buck takes the glass. He takes a big sip before anyone can warn him.

"Whoa Lordy, that's mighty strong," he sputters, as he sprays cider on his boots.

All three women laugh heartily. Victoria says, "Sorry, I thought all cowboys drank their cider hard."

"No, no, it's okay," he replies as he wipes his mouth on his shirt sleeve. He takes a deep breath and tries another, smaller sip.

"Guess I was expecting Mrs. Murphy's cider, hers wasn't so . . . potent. Hey, but this is plenty tasty." He continues to sip at his drink.

"Damn well better be the best cider you ever tasted," Victoria demands.

Victoria hands Vee a glass and takes one for herself. She sits in one of the empty seats. Monica comes back from the rail and does likewise. All three sit silently and look out over the fields.

Buck leans against the rail and considers them. They seem so confident but still he wonders if they really know what they are getting into.

"So, you obviously understand ag, but you know a lot of people have tried lots of different ideas to bring farming back. Not many of them have worked."

Victoria nearly jumps out of her chair as she exclaims, "Oh honey, we may be crazy but we're not stupid. She takes a long sip of cider and leans back. We are all about local. I've already presold our first order of barramundi to Tom's Bunkhouse downtown. Once the people in this town taste locally sourced seafood, they'll be hooked."

Monica chimes in without missing a beat. "We're already regulars at the farmers' market."

"Triple V brand tomatoes are top sellers," Victoria declares.

"We think the time is right for local community ag to finally take off, again. If we can get the rest of the farmers around here to work together. That's the dream," Vee adds.

Buck raises his glass and smiles at them. "Well, here's to big dreams."

"And good neighbors," Vee adds slyly.

They raise their glasses and toast.

Vee reaches down and picks Buck's hat up off the floor. It's a soggy crumpled mess. She crosses to the rail and holds it out to him. "Guess we owe you a new hat."

Buck reaches towards the hat and their hands touch. His fingers linger on hers before he takes the hat and inspects it. He grins as he tries to work it back into shape and then puts it on his head. It looks almost like a hat again. A stream of water drips down his face.

All three women laugh. He takes the hat off and gives it a sniff. "This old thing's been through worse. The smell will be gone in a week or two." He sits the hat on the rail. "Till then, it will be a reminder of my first ever big fish round-up."

Vee leans in closer to him. "You make a pretty good fish herder."

"For a cowboy." Victoria has the last word.

All four laugh and sip cider as the sun sets over the high plains.

Archie's Apology

Heck, my grandparents lived in the 'country.' I have fond memories of visiting the old farm place when I was a kid. We would run through the fields, play with the animals, fish in the pond. It was all great fun.

We didn't intentionally set out to destroy that way of life. Industrial agriculture was just the most efficient way to maximize profits in a world where people had better things to do than grow their own food. We were giving the customers what they wanted—convenience and low prices.

I understand why those folks who got left behind in failing rural communities felt like they had been robbed of their future. Frankly, they just weren't our problem. We were focused on the bigger picture: shipping the most products to the most consumers.

As technology became ever more dominant in all aspects of life, it seemed that our connection to the natural world might be lost forever in a sea of digital noise. Then, subtly at first, the tide shifted. No one abandoned their digital lifestyle, but more and more people became interested in the source of their food. We saw it as just another marketing opportunity and started slapping the words "all natural" on everything.

Ironically, this movement began in the cities where locally sourced food became the darling of hipster restaurants. Urban farmers' markets introduced a new generation to the thrill of hunting down food in the wild. As urban ex-pats migrated to rural communities, they brought these ideas back to the places where they had originated. They were not greeted with open arms. There was plenty of skepticism, which we played up, that this was just another attempt by outsiders to impose their values on the locals.

This new wave of craft farmers worked to rebuild the spirit of cooperation that had been the bedrock of agrarian communities before they had gotten hollowed out. This new generation of farmers realized that working together was the only chance they had against the power of our giant agricultural industry. They slowly began to be accepted as people realized they offered the only hope for forgotten rural communities. Even as the movement grew, they were more a distraction than a source of real competition. That is until Mother Nature stepped in.

A wave of monocrop disasters, made worse by rising temperatures and changing climates, exposed the vulnerability of our factory farms. They were just too big to adapt to a climate out of control. Some of the biggest names in agriculture just closed the barn doors and walked away. We lost close to 100 million acres of farmland in less than a decade. We were heading toward the very real possibility of widespread shortages and food riots.

It turned out that the network the small farmers had built helped them to thrive during this time. They were able to adapt season to season. They found ways to help each other when unexpected droughts or massive floods threatened. The days of low-cost, and yes, admittedly low-quality foodstuff, were replaced by small farmers working together to provide nutritious food to their local communities. They helped us avoid the agricultural apocalypse.

This new generation of farmers combined the best of traditional techniques with the latest technology. They used low-cost sensors and advanced monitoring systems to grow more food without extensive pesticides and chemicals. Their farms were powered by renewable energy. They even became major players in the re-greening of the countryside. Land we had abandoned was put back into use growing crops that helped pull carbon from the atmosphere.

Of course, there was only so much these local farms could do to support our national food needs. The most innovative techniques they created spread back to urban and suburban communities. Quarter-acre farms popped up across suburbia, and community gardens filled empty urban lots. Those new ideas helped to avert the food crisis that had seemed inevitable.

We are rapidly returning to being a nation of growers and harvesters.

9

Reimagining Sustainability

Gabby in Paradise

Gabby rushed through the kitchen and burst out the door, nearly knocking her mother over. She paused to look out over the horizon. Her home, like all the homes in Bahía del Paraíso, sat high in the air; protected from the floods that were a regular part of life in their small coastal community. From her perch, she could easily see all the way to the bay. In the early morning sunlight, the mangroves that grew along the water's edge glowed as if they were on fire. Beyond them, the crystal-clear blue water sparkled.

There had been a storm the night before. Not a very big one. The kind that Pipo dismissed as nothing more than a *pequeño mosquito* before going back to playing dominos with uncle Eduardo. But even small storms could leave behind unexpected treasures, so it was definitely worth checking out.

The houses on Gabby's street were connected by a series of walkways and swinging bridges. Tía Maria, one of the designers of the community, liked to remind everyone that these had not been part of the original plan. At first, she had been adamantly opposed. She declared that "flimsy bridges" would completely compromise the integrity of her carefully planned resilient design.

Everyone understood the importance of strong homes, but these were practical people. They argued that it made no sense to have to climb down twenty-eight steps and then right back up just to visit the next-door neighbor. *What about the old people,* they had cried? *Or the mothers with little children?*

Tía Maria and the planning committee finally gave in, but only after they had come up with a design that made it possible to detach the bridges whenever a hurricane approached. Gabby, like all the kids in the neighborhood, was just glad they had them. Scampering from house to house made her feel like a creature living high in the trees of an exotic jungle.

Gabby had recently turned thirteen. Like so many girls her age, she had experienced a growth spurt that left her tall and gangly. She navigated the swinging walkways with the loose grace of a child on the brink of becoming a confident young woman for whom every day would be a new adventure.

Her partner in those adventures was Danh. Even though they were the same age, she was nearly a head taller than him. Where she was lean and willowy, he was solid and compact. But he was one of the few boys her age who could keep up with her. They never missed the chance to search for treasures after a storm.

Danh's house was just a block away. It didn't take long for Gabby to get there. Standing on the deck that surrounded the house, she peered inside his open bedroom window and called out quietly, "Danh, you awake?"

" 'Bout time, *em gái,* " his booming response came from behind.

Startled, she spun around to see Danh, floating on his hover-board, a few feet away from the edge of the deck.

"Jerk," she said and swatted playfully at him.

He deftly maneuvered the board out of reach and smiled.

"Race you down," he challenged and then disappeared as he sent the board into a steep dive.

Gabby ran for the stairs. She hit every third step on the way down, getting to the bottom as fast as she could, where a smirking Danh leaned casually against the rail.

"You cheat," she complained.

"You just hate that you're too klutzy to fly a board."

Danh stepped forward and gave her a tentative hug, followed by an awkward moment; neither was sure what came next.

"I can still beat you in a fair race" Gabby shouted suddenly. She dashed off toward the water.

Danh watched her go and then hopped on his board. It didn't take him long to catch up. He slowed to match her pace, and the two of them followed the paths that zigzagged through the greenspace that separated the homes from the bay.

Tía Maria, who liked to explain everything, had told Gabby that this area was a critical part of the ecosystem. It provided the open land they needed for rainwater to run off and to slow the massive storm surges. Whatever the grown-up purpose might have been, it was the perfect place for the neighborhood kids to spend their days—running, playing, and exploring.

Gabby and Danh startled a flock of birds, and the sky suddenly filled with wildly flapping wings. The turbulence created by the frightened birds made Danh lose his balance, and he had to scramble to avoid crashing. They laughed and continued to make their way through the scrub.

When they finally reached the beach, Gabby dropped to the sand, out of breath. Danh circled her a couple of times before stepping off the board. The board idled by his side, ready to follow wherever he went. After a few deep gulps of air, Gabby sat up and surveyed the beach.

"I already did a zoom-by. Nothing interesting," Danh offered.

"Bummer," Gabby replied.

That was life as a storm pirate. Most of the time you only found little odds and ends, usually from the homes destroyed when the old barrier islands disappeared. Sometimes you got lucky and scored major treasure. Earlier in the summer, after a particularly big storm, they had discovered an ancient-looking log floating just offshore. Gabby's mother told them it looked like part of a Bodhi tree and that it might have been carried by the storm all the way from the Ivory Coast of Africa.

They had debated long and hard before deciding what to do with their newfound treasure. It was a point of pride among the community to reuse everything, even trash blown in by the storms. There was even an official village club called the *Remakers*, composed of artisans and hobbyists who repurposed the found objects into works of art, benches, and even playground structures that dotted the village.

Danh had imagined the log would make an impressive totem pole, but Gabby argued for something useful. In the end, they had compromised. With the help of Danh's dad, the best carver in the village, they turned the log into a bench with an intricately detailed scene telling the story of the Bodhi tree. It quickly became known around the neighborhood as Gabby and Danh's private place. They *had* been spending a lot of time there lately.

Even though they didn't expect to find anything nearly as exciting today, they still decided to walk the beach. The tide was going out, so they wandered among the mangroves—primordial trees with twisted roots and trunks dipping in and out of the water. Gabby and Danh meandered along until they came to the village's picnic pavilion. Their bench was just beyond it, tucked discretely next to a stand of bamboo that swayed in the breeze.

Soon, the park would fill up with young children and their parents, grandparents doing morning yoga, and teenagers looking for a spot to study or just hang out. For now, it belonged exclusively to Gabby and Danh. They sat down on the bench, close enough that their knees touched. The feeling sent a tiny tingle up Gabby's spine.

"So, whadya doing today?" she asked.

Danh, apparently completely unaware of the physical tension in the air replied nonchalantly, "Your aunt has me helping her build another one of her biodigesters."

Gabby laughed. "I warned you about asking Tía Maria to be your mentor. Once she gets hold of you, there's no getting away."

Danh pulled a handful of leaves off the bamboo growing next to the bench. He began weaving them together as they talked.

"It's kinda cool, making gas from food scraps and poop."

"Eh, gross," Gabby wrinkled her nose and frowned.

"As your aunt likes to say, 'you carry enough energy in your gut to power the entire planet,' " he replied as he continued to weave the leaves together.

Gabby hit Danh's knee with hers. "Now you're just trying to be disgusting."

Danh finished twisting the leaves together and held up an intricately woven bamboo ring. He handed it to Gabby and said; "All part of the great circle of life, em gái."

She took it from him and just stared at it. What was this supposed to mean? Was Danh giving her a ring? Or was it just another one of his goofy jokes?

The biodigesters Danh was helping build were the perfect low-tech solution to getting rid of all sorts of organic waste. They were really just waste composters designed to trap the gas that the decaying organic matter gave off. The gas could be used for cooking or heating and it was cleaner and less dangerous than any commercial natural gas.

The biodigesters were just one of the many renewable energy sources that powered the village. All of the roofs were covered in solar shingles, and most of the windows generated solar energy. There were a dozen big windmills off the coast, built to withstand two-hundred-mile-an-hour winds, and even a brand new blue energy system that used the power of the changing tides to create even more electricity.

The village owned all of the energy systems except for the windmills. Those had been built by a green energy co-op that shared the power with the village in exchange for the rights to locate the windmills in the bay.

Altogether, they produced more than enough energy for all the community's needs, even enough to recharge the electric hoverboard that followed Danh everywhere. Best of all, according to Pipo, the new energy sources didn't get destroyed every time there was a storm.

"So, 'bout you?" Danh asked.

"Aqua harvest with Mom." Gabby's mother managed the community's aquafarm. The village's aquafarm was one of its most successful projects, providing food for the residents and a source of income. In part, this success was an unanticipated byproduct of the way they had redesigned the village's landscape. Instead of the traditional lawns growing non-native grasses, the village was filled with ground covers that naturally flourished in a salty, coastal environment. As a result, there was no need for fertilizers that used to run off into the bay and cause deadly algae blooms.

The water in the bay was cleaner than it had been in over a hundred years. With a little help from local marine biologists, it had been easy to re-establish the oyster and scallop beds and bring back the fish and shrimp populations. The return of the seafood harvests was a reminder of what had brought many of Gabby's and Danh's ancestors to this coast originally. Today, that natural bounty was enhanced by the latest sustainable aquafarming methods, and the village was once again a prime supplier of fresh seafood to the surrounding region.

Working with her Mom, Gabby could earn badges in marine biology and aqua-ag. She thought she might even do a little marine science one day. For now, she mainly liked hanging out with her mother.

The community wasn't self-reliant when it came to just seafood; it was filled with vegetable gardens ranging in size from box gardens that lined the community pathways where anyone could pick a handful of herbs to cook with to a state-of-the-art aeroponics greenhouse. Inside the greenhouse, vegetables literally grew in the air, their bare roots hanging down like stringy hair. Between the year-round warm weather and cutting-edge agriculture technology, the community produced more than enough food to feed itself and to send to nearby markets.

"Oh, hey. S'posed to ask if you want to come to Pipo's birthday party on Friday. It's his eightieth, so Mom and Tía Maria are fixing all traditional stuff."

"For sure," Danh exclaimed. "I mean if it's cool with you and all."

Gabby tried to respond nonchalantly. "Whatever, it's nice to have somebody my age around, you know. They may even make *ropa vieja*. Its Pipo's favorite and Mom said she knew you liked it."

"With real beef? Last time your mom made that, I pigged out. Kinda surprised she'd invite me back."

"Oh, she thinks you're special." Gabby smiled.

In fact, Sophia and Tía Maria had taken to referring to Danh as Gabby's "special friend." Gabby wasn't sure how she felt about that. Oh, she knew their relationship was way different than she had with any of her other friends, but that didn't mean she wanted her mother to be broadcasting it to everyone.

They spent the next few minutes sitting in silence, something they often did. At first these pauses felt awkward, but lately Gabby had realized that they were special moments—sharing the natural beauty of this place they were so lucky to call home.

Their reverie was interrupted by the arrival of Pipo, out for his morning walk. He rarely missed a day and always wore the same outfit—a perfectly pressed guayabera shirt, linen slacks, and his trademark Panama hat. He stopped when he saw them.

"Why are you niños not in school?" he demanded.

Gabby blushed and tried to explain to him, for the hundredth time, that it was not like the old days when sitting in a classroom was the only place you could learn. Gabby and her friends learned everywhere. She even tried to explain to Pipo how her friend Kim, who lived in Shanghai, was teaching her Mandarin. In exchange for language lessons, Gabby was teaching Kim how to draw. Just because her teacher was her age didn't mean it was easy. She would still have to prove mastery if she wanted to earn the language badge. Pipo should know by now how much Gabby loved earning badges. She had more than most kids her age. There were plenty of resources to help her, available anywhere, anytime. Many were even free.

When she had finally finished her explanation, Pipo shook his head in bewilderment. "Come walk with me, *nieta*."

Gabby gave Danh a quick look and got up. "So, see you Friday, here in the park."

"It's a date," he replied, hopping off the bench. When he realized what he had said, he stammered quickly, "Gotta fly. Got poop to scoop. Catch you later." With that, he jumped on the hoverboard and zipped off.

She watched him disappear. A voice in her head was shrieking: *A date? Is that really what he had said?* She wasn't sure if she was confused, excited, or both. She was so distracted, she didn't even notice that Pipo had continued his walk without her.

She ran to catch up and took his hand as they walked toward the shore. Pipo began to reminisce. Walking with one of his grandchildren and telling them stories of the past was his favorite thing to do. Gabby was frequently his audience, and she had heard most of his stories many times.

"You know, Gabriela, we use to live right here on this very spot. Our home wasn't fancy, but it had been in our family for seven generations, ever since our people first came here to fish. It was not an easy life, but our people were strong and worked hard. Your family helped to build a tiny fishing village into this community.

"We raised all of our children here. Maria, Sophia, Carlito, and Eduardo all grew up here. So many wonderful memories." His voice wavered, and the old man paused to collect himself before he continued.

"Then came the summer of the great storms. Six hurricanes in less than three months. It seemed like we spent all our time getting ready for a storm or cleaning up after one; sometimes doing both at the same time. The last storm, the biggest one of all, hit right here. The entire village washed away. *Destruido*. Your abuela cried and cried for days."

Gabby fought to keep back her tears. The thought of her tiny little grandmother losing everything made her so sad every time she heard this story, even though she knew it had a happy ending.

Over the years, life after the storms had developed into a predictable pattern. First came the clean-up, sometimes taking weeks or months, then the insurance companies and the government would help them rebuild. But this time the insurance companies didn't come. They said there had been too many storms and they were out of money. The state's catastrophe fund was empty, and there were no funds available from the federal government. For the first time, the residents didn't know how they were going to rebuild.

That's when Tía Maria came home. She had been working up north as an urban planner. Under her leadership, a group of homeowners approached the city with a bold plan. In exchange for assistance in building new homes, the citizens would turn over their land along the shore. Everyone agreed that the old ways weren't going to work anymore, especially as the sea levels continued to rise and the warmer ocean waters spawned more violent storms.

Still, there weren't many in local government who could imagine how this joint private/public partnership would work. After months of negotiations, the officials learned what Gabby's family had long known; you don't argue with Tía Maria. And that was how Bahía del Paraíso was born.

First, they had scraped the site of the old village clean. What remained of the buildings that had once crowded the coast were bulldozed over. Where there had been concrete, mangroves were planted. All the area along the shore was given back to the bay.

In exchange for the coastline property, the residents were given vacant farmland next to the former village. The land—long ago over-farmed and abandoned—had been considered worthless. But when Tía Maria got her hands on it, she got to work building a world class resilient village.

Every building was elevated to avoid damage from floods. They used smartbricks with carbon nanofibers to build walls that could withstand a cat 5 hurricane. Gabby wasn't sure she totally understood how the walls worked, but she knew she felt safe and secure in her bedroom, even when the big winds were blowing. Tía Maria also insisted the community be environmentally sustainable. Along with all the renewal energy, they built an advanced rainwater collection and recycling system.

In just a couple years, the community exceeded their goal of having a zero-carbon footprint. In fact, they could show that the community had a net positive effect on their environment, making the water and air cleaner than they had been before. Most importantly for everyone who lived there, the cost of living in the new village was a lot less than it had been in the old one.

Important people from around the world came to visit them now. Bahía del Paraíso was designated an official United Nation's sustainable development site, and Tía Maria was always invited to important conferences to tell their story.

Pipo stopped walking. Gabby knew they had reached his favorite spot on the beach. Just fifty yards offshore, an enormous, brightly-colored sea dragon rose out of the water. It was without a doubt the most unique sculpture in the village. The dragon's scales were made from ceramic tiles, salvaged from Pipo's old home. The tiles had been brought all the way from Cuba by Gabby's ancestors.

"You know Gabriella, everything in our new village is so

incredible. Our lives have never been better. But we must not forget those who brought us to this place."

Gabby agreed it was pretty neat that something from her family's past was now part of her future. What was even cooler to a thirteen-year-old was the fact that some industrious volunteers had rigged the dragon up to use gas from a biodigester to breathe real fire. Of course, Tía Maria only allowed them to use it for special occasions.

Gabby knew there was a good chance they would light the dragon for Pipo's birthday party. She imagined the scene. The dragon that represented her family, breathing fire under a star-filled sky, moonlight reflecting off the water. That might just be the perfect time and place for a first kiss.

Archie's Apology

Man, did we ever get tired of hearing about climate change! The tree huggers and greenies just wouldn't let it go. Oh, it wasn't that we doubted the science, we knew the studies were right. It was the economics that terrified us.

We had spent a century building an economy powered by fossil fuels, and we had no idea how to turn that around and maintain our place at the top of the profit pyramid. It was true, we were rushing headlong toward a catastrophe that could destroy everything we had built, we just couldn't imagine how to slow it down.

So, we did what we did best. We unleashed the power of our corporate PR machines to distract the public from what was really happening. For a while it worked. Temperatures kept rising, the weather kept getting more extreme, coastal cities flooded; but we just kept sowing doubt about the real causes. We even managed to turn the discussion into a political issue and effectively shut down almost all reasoned debate about climate change and energy policy.

During the late teens and early twenties, some cities and even a couple states tried to step into the regulatory void. They divested their pension funds from fossil fuel companies and established carbon taxes. The big energy companies met every new regulation with renewed propaganda. They filled the media with stories of lost jobs, economic disaster, and warned of the total collapse of our way of life. Our best weapon was fear.

By the twenties, it seemed as if we had reached a stalemate. The evidence that we were seriously damaging our planet and threatening the lives of those who lived on it keep building. At the same time, the big powers; the large energy companies and governments were locked in a continuing battle that seemed guaranteed to block any real solutions.

Who broke through the logjam? Individuals, frustrated with having to pay the very real costs, decided to take matters into their own hands. At first it was a loosely connected movement of individuals trying new ways to drop off the grid and live more sustainable lives. As their ideas gained popularity they began to establish eco-villages. These intentional communities were dedicated to showing that it was possible to eliminate almost all forms of pollution by using renewals, reducing, recycling, and reusing. We scoffed, but they continued to innovate. By the end of the twenties, their so-called radical ideas became commonplace practice. Communities across the country began to adopt some of the more innovative technologies.

A big part of their success came from reframing the discourse. Instead of focusing on the things that people had to give up to save the environment, they promoted the positive benefits. More and more people realized that it was possible to own their climate footprint and make a positive contribution without giving up on their way of life. This new climate awareness gave rise to a radical shift in the larger conversation. Calls for living in harmony with the planet finally transcended old divides and became a unifying meme.

The ripples from the shift created a new form of economics—*net positive environomics*. This new model demanded that every consumption decision had to benefit people and the environment. A renewed partnership between people and the planet was born. Everyone began to understand our future survival required giving back to the natural world. For those of us who had long believed this was our private garden to plunder as we pleased, this was a hard lesson to learn.

10

Reimagining Community

The Birth of Hope

The pillow vibrated gently at first and then more insistently. Jason finally opened his eyes and struggled through the fog of deep sleep. He reached for his glasses on the bedside table and clumsily put them on. With a blink he activated the clock function and the time appeared on his lenses. What he saw made him blink a second time. *What the heck?* he thought. Why was his alarm going off at 5:45? As he struggled to put together the pieces of the puzzle, he heard his wife Sarah moaning from her side of the bed.

"Oh, god, oh god, oh god," Sarah whispered through clenched teeth.

Jason was suddenly fully awake. He sat bolt upright and turned to check on Sarah. She was stretched out next to him, the bedsheet covering her protruding belly, her face contorted in pain.

"What? Are you—is it—?" he stammered.

Sarah expelled a long sharp breath. "It's time."

Jason jumped out of the bed. "What do I need to do? Should I call Harriet?"

Slowly and carefully, Sarah pulled herself up. Strands of her long blonde hair fell over her face. She blew the hair out of her eyes and took a measured breath. "Dear, come here."

Jason made his way to her side of the bed. Sarah reached out and took his hand.

"Everything is under control. Harriet is already on her way. She got pinged when I had the first contraction. She'll be here in a few minutes. Until then I need you to . . . " Sarah clenched her teeth as another wave of contractions hit. In between the pains, she finished her thought. "Help me stay calm. Oh god."

Jason sat next to Sarah on the bed and tried desperately to remember the techniques they had learned in pregnancy class. The best he could do was follow Sarah's lead as she took long slow measured breaths. Between every breath, he checked the time projected on his glasses, but that feeling of complete helplessness kept returning. Why couldn't he remember what they had practiced? He and Sarah had even rehearsed the birth day in virtual reality during their classes. Now, he had no idea what he was supposed to do. He felt like his brain had been wiped clean. As the seconds ticked by, Jason tried to focus, tried to remain calm, tried not to hyperventilate. He was pretty sure he was on the verge of failing all three tasks when the door to the bedroom swung open and a stout grandmotherly figure, with long grey hair pulled back in a pony tail, hustled into the room.

"It's time, Luv!" Harriet shouted in glee, as she dropped her ancient bag on the floor and crossed the room to check on her patient. She laid a hand on Sarah's belly and gently poked and prodded. Her movements were so practiced and smooth that even Jason could feel her calm authority filling the room.

As Harriet fussed over Sarah, her apprentice, Diego, stood just inside the doorway. He was seventeen, tall, thin as a rail, and as reserved as Harriet was outgoing. He had been working with Harriet for nearly a year now, and she told everyone in town that he was going to be an excellent midwife one day soon. Harriet also insisted on introducing the two of them as Mutt and Jeff to everyone they met, a reference that despite all her efforts to explain never made any sense to the young man. He watched her every move carefully, waiting for the sign that she needed his assistance.

"Let's make you comfortable, Dear, we're going to be here for a while," Harriet said to Sarah.

Diego silently moved to the other side of the bed and scooped up Jason's pillow. He gently pulled the sheet and covers off Sarah and slipped the pillow under her knees. When he finished, he carefully pulled the sheet back up.

Harriett finished fussing over Sarah and turned to Jason. She smiled as she recognized the look of sheer terror on his face.

"Now, Dear, take a deep breath and relax. We've got at least four hours before the main event."

Sarah motioned for Jason. "Come here, Babe."

Jason slipped past Harriet and took his wife's outstretched hand.

"Why don't you go downstairs? You know people are going to be dropping by all morning. Somebody has to entertain them."

Jason started to protest but Sarah cut him off. "It was the plan, right? We'll call you when it's time. I promise I won't have our baby without you."

Jason turned to Harriett for backup. The older woman pulled an ancient aromatherapy diffuser from her bag and tossed it across the room to Diego. She turned to Jason.

"This is all just pregame. You'll be here for the kickoff."

Jason knew he couldn't talk Sarah out of her decision; he'd tried when she had first told him that she didn't expect him to stand around all day waiting for her to go into labor. He bent over his wife and gave her a quick kiss.

Harriett gave them just a moment before she hustled Jason out of the bedroom. Diego closed the door silently behind him.

Jason called up Sarah's health metrics on his wrist pad and synced them to his display. Now, no matter what he was doing, he would be able to monitor her breathing, heartbeat, and even blood pressure, displayed on the corner of his glasses. If anything unusual happened, he would be alerted. He texted SARAH I LOVE YOU with a heart-shaped emoji and headed downstairs.

The house Sarah and Jason lived in had been built in the late 1980s, during one of the many housing booms that had rolled through the small town over the past fifty years. This neighborhood had been part of a short-lived gentrification attempt, replacing the neat and tidy homes built in the nineteen twenties with ostentatious McMansions.

Today the house, like most in the neighborhood, was dual use. Jason and Sarah lived on the second floor. The rest of the house was taken up by the offices of their business, the *Weekly Gazette*.

Jason wandered through the empty great room that served as the primary workspace for the *Weekly*'s staff. In a few hours it would be filled with activity as reporters, editors, and designers came and went, held story meetings, planned community events, and argued over which articles should be uploaded to the newsfeed immediately and which should be held for the weekly print edition.

Jason headed for the downstairs bedroom that had been converted into an office that Sarah and Jason shared with Megan, their editor-in-chief. Each had a desk facing one wall. A large paper-thin computer screen hung on the fourth wall. The middle of the room was prime real estate for piles of newspapers, flyers, and posters. Jason picked his way past the clutter and plopped down at his desk. He randomly rearranged a few papers, stacking and unstacking them for no reason. He considered checking the *Weekly*'s online newsfeed but couldn't imagine being able to focus.

He blinked, and Sarah's vitals expanded to fill his lens. He stared at each beat of her heart and unconsciously began to synch his breathing to her rhythm. The process helped to calm him. Finally, he forced himself to minimize the image and direct his attention elsewhere.

His gaze landed on the framed map on the wall in front of his desk. The parchment map in its heavy gold frame hung on the wall directly in front of Jason's desk. Throughout Sarah's pregnancy, Jason had found himself spending more and more time contemplating the map.

CRAS QUI SOMNIUM VIDISSE SE FAVET was written in flowing script across the bottom. Jason had learned from Google that the words translate into English as *Tomorrow favors a dreamer*. The map was an original from 1502, the first to include reference to the discovery of a new continent, denoted simply as *Nuovo Monda*, the New World.

It had been a gift from Sarah. She'd bought it for him back in the days when they could still afford such an extravagant purchase and told him that she hoped it would inspire him to always dream about the brightest possible tomorrows.

Jason had always been intrigued by the map's detail. It was as if the mapmaker had personally visited every part of the world he had drawn. Of course, that would have been impossible in his day. The mapmaker would have had to rely on the stories of those faraway lands brought back by sailors and explorers.

For those parts of the world still undiscovered in his time, the mapmaker had used his imagination to create intricate details. Beyond the New World, there was an ocean filled with gigantic fish, mermaids, and sea dragons. This *Terra Incognito* seemed as real to the mapmaker as the streets of sixteenth-century Venice must have been. Those details gave the map its power. The images transformed it from being merely a record of past journeys into a story of future possibility. Those stories had compelled thousands of men to climb aboard rickety wooden ships and sail off toward unknown lands, to face sea monsters and who knew what else, in search of a better tomorrow.

Jason, sitting at his desk five centuries later, still felt the power of that possibility. In his and Sarah's case, it was no longer unexplored lands across vast oceans, but now the ever-changing landscape of a world buffeted by technological change.

Thinking of Sarah, he checked her vitals again. Everything was fine, just like she had promised him it would be. He began to silently count her heartbeats and repeated the breathing exercise. It was going to be a long morning but relying on data was second nature to Jason.

Like so many bright middle-class digital natives, he had grown up immersed in technology. His mother was a civil engineer. His father was a Rwandan intellectual who escaped the genocide and served on the faculty of Columbia University. They had taught their son to work hard, follow his passion, and make a difference. For Jason that had meant playing with computers from an early age. He spent his summers at computer camps and attended the most rigorous private schools. By the time he was ready for college, studying computer science was the easy choice. In the early twenties, it was still considered the fastest ticket to *the good life*. That was before AI started writing software. But when Jason made his choice, all he saw was that the geeks were the ones with the nice cars, fancy condos, and expensive vacations. You could even make enough to afford a family, if that was your dream.

Jason graduated near the top of his class. Even before getting his degree he had offers from all the top digital companies. He turned down Facebook, Google, Amazon and the other Silicon Valley stalwarts. To Jason and most of his peers, these once savvy pioneers had become the factory owners of the knowledge economy. The real action was with the new generation of start-ups in one of the literally hundreds of *Silicon Alleys* popping up across the country. Jason signed with one near Boston.

The biggest prize for a start-up software company was to build the killer authenticity algorithm. Social media had drowned out all the traditional media outlets and in the process, had torn down all the old standards of fair and accurate reporting. The result was lots of noise and less and less useful content.

The technology behind the social media sites compounded the problem. Those stories that got shared most were pushed to even more users. Quantity of likes replaced quality, truthfulness became irrelevant. Muckraking, rumors, and outright lies dominated most of the social media news sites.

A backlash had already begun. People were either retreating into their own information bubbles, where their beliefs were never challenged, or dropping out of social media altogether. The big media players were starting to panic as they saw their market share erode. Everyone had become fixated on creating algorithms that would deliver balanced and accurate news.

The best algorithms could meet the authenticity goal almost 70 percent of the time, but no one seemed to be having any luck increasing that number and guaranteeing a balanced feed to every user. The company that reached the goal first would see their valuation soar into the billions.

Jason had met Sarah his first day of work. She was leading the team assigned to create the authenticity algorithm. He fell for her almost immediately. Not only was Sarah a world-class software designer, but she was also athletic and gorgeous. She'd grown up outdoors in southern California and loved sports, but what she really loved was organizing people.

Sarah didn't make a habit of dating guys at work; most of them were too intimidated by her. Jason was different. He was quiet, but confident. It didn't hurt that he was really good looking and was interested in the world beyond technology.

Sarah was pleasantly surprised when Jason asked her out for coffee. They started hanging out, and it wasn't long before they were a couple.

They worked hard and partied even harder. Everyone was young and making money faster than they could spend it. The investors behind the company were lavish in rewarding their top performers. Sarah and Jason raked in the bonuses and perks.

Then, without warning, it all came tumbling down. An open-source software collective was the first to successfully create the accuracy algorithm that could deliver a balanced feed of authenticated news items to users. The day after announcing their success, they released all their code for free.

Overnight, Sarah and Jason went from eating handcrafted artisan pizzas, delivered by UberEatsGrubHub drones, to nuking frozen discs from the corner CVS. Jason and Sarah, powered in part by the energy of young love, embraced this chance to reimagine their future. They spent long evenings brainstorming ideas for their next great adventure.

They were sitting on the floor of Sarah's living room one night finishing off the last bottle of their expensive wine collection when Sarah tapped on her wrist pad and pulled up a website. She tapped again to send the image to the big screen hanging on the wall of the apartment.

"Okay, so here's a wild idea," she said tentatively.

Onscreen was an ad for a local newspaper for sale in a small southern town that Jason had never heard of before.

Jason just stared at the image, not sure what to think.

"Wait, are you saying we should buy a newspaper?

"It's super cheap," she replied.

"Yeah because no one reads newspapers anymore."

"Wait, hear me out." Sarah leaned in close and continued. "Most of the major newsfeeds are celebrity clickbait, political propaganda, or designed to scrape data for retailers. Even with the accuracy algorithms, real news—especially local news—is dead. But people still need that. Local newspapers used to bind communities together. There's a hunger out there. I can sense it. You've seen the growth of neighborhood social media sites. What if we could build a local platform based on trust that delivered news and encouraged community dialogue?"

"What does that have to do with buying a newspaper?"

Sarah, excited, hopped to her feet. "We'd expand the digital site. Use the open source code to deliver an objective and balanced news feed responsive to the community. Lots of people are talking about creating new forms of journalism. We could be the ones to do it."

Jason looked unconvinced. "In the middle of nowhere?"

Sarah bent down toward him. "What have we got to lose? It's not like there are gonna be a lot of high paying jobs out there for coders."

Jason put down his wine glass and considered what Sarah was suggesting. On the one hand, she was right. In the past couple of years, the entire software field had been turned upside down. Artificial intelligence had advanced so fast that more and more software was writing itself. There was already a glut of unemployed coders. Many of them were working for free with open source co-ops. That meant even fewer companies willing to invest in hiring full-time software designers.

Sarah could see that he was starting to come around. She refilled his wine glass and handed it to him.

"We might actually be doing work that mattered," she offered.

"Yeah, but this kinda sounds like purpose without any chance of making a profit."

"Tomorrow favors a dreamer." She raised her glass in a toast. He raised his own. They clinked glasses and drank. Sarah sat down next to him and sealed the deal with a kiss. Their voyage in search of a new world had begun.

The smell of freshly brewed coffee pulled Jason back to reality, and he got up to see who was in the kitchen. He checked Sarah's vitals as he went. Everything looked good. Her breathing and heart rates were normal. Her blood pressure was probably lower than his.

Jason found Megan in the kitchen, busily preparing breakfast for the staff. Along with being editor-in-chief, she ruled over the company kitchen. The *Weekly*, like most digital start-ups, was part workplace, part commune, so having an accomplished chef on staff was a real plus. Megan was a little older than Jason and Sarah, a mother with two young kids, but could easily keep up with the youngest of the staff. Megan was born and raised in the town. Her family had arrived from Ireland in the early 1800s and proudly claimed to be among the first residents. She was cracking eggs into a giant mixing bowl when Jason entered.

"Hey, Soon-to-be-Dad. I figured you could use some coffee." Megan gestured toward the industrial size coffee urn and went back to cracking the eggs.

Jason poured himself a cup and sat down at the counter. He watched as Megan poured the eggs into a massive frying pan. Her fiery red hair flew around her face as she worked.

"You didn't have to come in so early." He blew across the cup of steaming coffee.

"You kidding me?" She wiped her long, freckled hands on a towel and smiled at Jason. "It's a big news day. The publishers of the *Weekly Gazette* are about to have their first kid. Everybody in town is waiting for updates." Megan laughed. She picked up a spatula and started to stir the eggs in the pan.

"Looks like you're planning to feed everybody in town too." Jason took a sip of his coffee.

"Hey, not my fault that everybody thinks the office is also a community center." Megan waved the spatula in the air to make her point.

"Blame Sarah for that, not me. You know I'm a coder geek; I don't even like people all that much."

"Lucky for you that Sarah does. If it wasn't for her, this would be one lonely operation." Megan leaned into the job of stirring the congealing mass of eggs.

Megan was right. Sarah had won over the local community from the first. She promised the former owners of the paper that they would keep the print edition for at least three more years.

Jason figured by then they would probably be broke and have to scuttle the whole project. He couldn't imagine that a physical paper would ever attract more than a dwindling number of older subscribers. At first, he was right. Every month the number of subscribers continued to drop. The declining numbers had nothing to do with the new owners. After years of steady economic decline, the town had suffered a major blow within weeks of Sarah and Jason's arrival. The giant poultry plant, the last major employer in the area, announced it was going to automate completely. More than 400 workers, most second- and third-generation Latinos, would soon be without jobs.

Before Sarah and Jason took over, the former owners of the paper had already laid off their small staff and were simply using the freely available software to search the internet for articles that met the interest parameters of the local community and reprinted or reposted them.

Sarah had a different idea. She insisted that their focus had to be on original, local news. Her insistence caused their very first serious argument. Jason was adamant that they couldn't afford to hire staff. Sarah refused to budge on her vision.

Fortunately for their marriage, and the *Weekly Gazette*, they came up with a compromise. They decided to run the company like a wiki. Sarah invited anyone in the community to become a contributing reporter. These volunteers would decide what stories were of interest and submit them. The entire group would have a say in approving any article. Once they had vetted a story, it would be reviewed for accuracy by the software. Only those articles that passed both the AI and the volunteers would get published.

It was an egalitarian idea that turned out to be completely impractical. The process did produce articles that were accurate, balanced, and relevant to the community, but it took *forever*. By the time an article finally made it into the weekly print edition, it was long past newsworthy.

Jason suggested that they change the name to the *Local Historian*. Sarah was not amused and instead hired Megan to be their editor-in-chief.

Megan was the perfect choice for the job. She was teaching English at the local high school when they brought her on. She had the patience to get the best out of her team of volunteer reporters and the discipline to make sure they met their deadlines.

The paper's circulation started to slowly grow. It turned out that lots of people liked the idea of a weekly newspaper. Slow news began to catch on. Local businesses signed on as sponsors. The website became an important source for up-to-the-minute news when needed. They were able to convert the volunteer staff into permanent co-owners of the company. Everyone was getting paid, at least a small salary. Sarah had been right.

Jason took another sip of his coffee and marveled at how lucky he was to have found such a perfect partner. She truly was an amazing woman, about to become an amazing mother.

Bryce, one of the younger reporters, came into the kitchen carrying a large paper bag. He plopped the bag on the kitchen counter. "Freida sends her love, and two dozen bagels." Bryce pulled a bagel with pink swirls and held it up for Megan and Jason to see. "She even baked a special birth-day bagel."

"Geez, is everybody in this town obsessed with the birth of our child?" Jason asked.

"Uh, yeah." Bryce took a bite out of the pink bagel. "Strawberry, not so bad."

"Apparently, you haven't checked the feed this morning." Bryce continued. "Sarah is trending number two, just behind the report on the accident at the Tri-City Windmill Farm."

"Seriously?" Jason called up the news feed on his glasses. Sure enough, there it was, trending number two on the *Weekly*'s site. There was even a poll comparing when the readers thought she would go into labor versus her health data prediction.

Megan scooped a pile of scrambled eggs onto a plate and slid it across the counter to him, as he clicked the image away with a shake of his head.

"Eat up—you're going to need your extrovert energy today, Boss," she told him.

Megan was right. Over the next couple hours, the office filled up with people. At first, it was mostly staff members wandering in. They congregated around the massive table, wolfed down breakfast, and brainstormed ideas for a special edition of the paper to commemorate the birth. Throughout the morning, they were joined by an assortment of local well-wishers. They came to drop off food, stay for a cup of coffee, and catch up with their neighbors. It seemed everyone was following Sarah's progress on the *Weekly* site and they all made a point of telling Jason how excited they were for them.

After a while, it started to get to be too much for him. He understood that Sarah felt the need to invite the community into every part of their life. For her it was part of being transparent. Jason could have used a little more privacy. All he wanted was to go back upstairs and be with her.

He was just about to excuse himself when Garrett Armstrong, the city's former long-time mayor, stepped through the open door. Garrett was in his late sixties, short and muscular, with close-cropped grey hair. He looked like the ex-marine he was. "Yo, Jason, can you give me a hand here?"

Garrett wrangled a wooden rocking chair toward the door. Jason joined him and it took both of them to maneuver it through the doorway. "Melanie says you guys probably already have one of those fancy hi-tech rocking chairs, but I wanted to offer this one to you and Sarah. It's been in our family for three generations. Meant to get it to you sooner, but it took me longer to refinish than I planned," Garrett explained.

Jason ran his hand over the intricately carved wood. "Wow, it's beautiful Garrett. Thank you. Hungry?"

"I could stand a little something," he said.

"You know where the kitchen is. We've got a ton of food."

Garrett gave Jason a fatherly pat on the shoulder and headed to the kitchen.

Garrett had become a regular at the *Weekly* since he'd lost the last mayoral election. He had been running against a younger opponent, a woman whose parents had originally come to town from Guatemala to work in the processing plants. She had been born in the town, grew up there, and came back after college to care for her recently unemployed parents.

The town's Latino migrant community had been supporting the fragile local economy with the wages they made at the processing plants. Now that those jobs were gone the economic stress was causing old resentments to resurface. The rhetoric during the campaign got pretty ugly. Some of the old-time residents made it clear that they considered the young woman an outsider, representative of those who wanted to take their town away from them. Nasty stories and rumors began to circulate on social media.

The *Weekly* strictly followed their policy, reporting accurately on both candidates and offering equal access to the opinion pages. They refused to print any opinion piece, including letters to the editor, that could not be substantiated. When the Mayor was defeated, many of his long-time supporters blamed the paper for swaying the election, even though it was clear they had remained non-partisan. Garrett responded by writing an open letter to the paper congratulating them on their fair and balanced reporting and calling them a real key to the town's future.

His endorsement was the opportunity Sarah was looking for. She invited Garrett to become the company's community liaison. He accepted immediately. They took over the high school auditorium for weekly meetings on everything from the economic situation to racial tensions. The new mayor gave the paper unlimited access to all town hall decisions. Sarah and Jason had to add even more staff to plan and organize community events. The town became more inclusive and the residents more optimistic about their future.

In part, these efforts worked because everyone felt like their voices were heard, but also because the town started to flourish again. Long abandoned storefronts reopened on Main Street. More run-down McMansions were turned into co-operative living and working spaces. Longtime residents and newcomers came together to start new businesses.

Jason stood by the front door watching his friends, neighbors, and coworkers celebrate the joy of being a part of something. He realized that he and Sarah had reached their own *New World*, and it felt right. Even though they were just a few hours away from sailing into the uncharted waters of parenthood, which terrified him, he knew they would have plenty of help.

He smiled, and then he started to drag the rocking chair toward the stairs. He figured he could use it as an excuse to check on Sarah. He made it as far as the third step when he felt a slight tingling at his temple. He blinked to accept the incoming call, and Diego appeared in his lenses.

"Ms. Harriet says you should probably come on up."

Jason put the rocker down immediately. As he was about to turn and vault up the steps, the chair started sliding down. Jason froze, not sure which way to go. Suddenly Garrett, sandwich in hand, sprinted across the room and caught the chair before it hit the floor. He casually took a bite out of his sandwich.

"Go, Son."

Jason flew up the stairs, two at a time.

Later that evening, Jason sat in the rocking chair, gently rocking their new daughter as Sarah slept peacefully in the bed. The baby opened her big blue eyes and cooed softly at him.

"Well hello there, Hope Elizabeth Strauss-Mangretsky. Did you know that you're already a local celebrity?" Jason held up the latest edition of the *Weekly Gazette*. "I hope you like being the center of attention."

On the front page was a close-up of the baby, taken just a couple of hours after she was born, eyes wide open and smiling in her mother's arms. Above it read the headline:

Hope is born.

Archie's Apology

They had hope.

We had power and money and control. We had data and marketing and knew how to manipulate the masses. We knew how to divide and create fear.

They had hope.

Hope that our true nature was to be generous and caring. Hope that most people wanted to belong to something bigger. Hope that dialogue could create community.

When the odds were the greatest they stepped forward and took the biggest risks. They embraced the tools of a new digital age to empower individuals, build businesses that put purpose over profit, and connect people across social, economic, and political spectrums.

They had hope.

And they used that hope to reimagine our tomorrows, to create a future that is sustainable, abundant and equitable.

Maybe, we should have had hope.

CONCLUSION

Cool Stories, Bro! So Now What?

I consider myself extremely lucky. I get to spend every day researching, thinking about, and imagining ways we can make the future better. The best part of my job is sharing stories of those optimistic tomorrows with others through speeches, workshops, and now this book. But I realize that most people don't have the same opportunity to devote all of their time to thinking about the future. I've left the stage more than once, fully aware that for many of the people in the audience, the stories I tell will become cocktail party filler. The ideas might be exciting, the escape from the negative news that dominates our media a welcome reprieve, but at the end of the day you have to get on with life, a life that is filled with day-to-day challenges. A life that doesn't leave much time for contemplating the future, much less creating it.

I began this book with the bold promise that I was going to help you create a future that doesn't suck. How exactly is that supposed to happen once you lay down your Kindle and return to your busy life? More to the point, what do you need to do next? My advice is simple; let the stories guide you.

Stories inform, inspire, and empower. The best do all three simultaneously, but each result plays a role in building a pathway to our better tomorrows. That path will be different for each of you. Here are some ideas about how you might use these strategic narratives in your personal quest.

Many of you will see these stories as interesting diversions or entertaining what-ifs, an easy way to consume information about the trends that will likely shape our futures. That's fine. The power of stories is that once released, they are impossible to contain. They spread organically. One of the effects of sharing scenarios like these is that they sharpen the reader's attention to those underlying trends. You'll find yourself noticing items in the news or on your social feed that reinforce the ideas shared here. Maybe it will be a report about a community working to spread digital empowerment to all its citizens or an entrepreneur building a business that benefits her profits and the planet. Being more attuned to these positive efforts is the first step toward building hope for better tomorrows.

The next time you encounter a story about the coming dystopian future, you'll read it differently. You will begin to question some of the assumptions. Then one day, you'll find yourself in a lively conversation about the threats of artificial intelligence, robots, or climate change. That's when it will happen. Without even thinking about it, you'll challenge those preconceived notions by suggesting that a better tomorrow is possible. You might go so far as to tell your version of one of these stories as an example. Congratulations! That's the moment you become an optimistic futurist. By sharing these stories, you will be laying the foundation for our better tomorrows.

These stories may inspire some of you. You may find in them an idea for a new project, motivation to change careers, or even your life's purpose. If these stories have touched you in this way, then I urge you to begin looking for other people who share your dreams. You will be surprised by the allies you find. Each of these stories was inspired by real people working today to create better tomorrows. The reference section at the end of the book can help you find some of those individuals and groups. Check them out, follow them, join them. If you can't find any nearby, start your own group of optimistic futurists.

Use these stories as a blueprint for your vision of the future. Start by digging deeper into the content and ask the hard questions:

HOW CAN I USE MY SKILLS AND TALENTS TO CONTRIBUTE TO THESE FUTURES?

WHAT MUST CHANGE FOR THESE TOMORROWS TO BE POSSIBLE?

WHOM DO I NEED TO HELP ME REALIZE MY VISION?

Your inspirations will be the springboard for building our better tomorrows.

Some of you will remain skeptical. You want to be part of a better future, but you're not sure if the versions presented here are the right ones for you. Maybe these particular stories don't resonate with your situation or dreams. Your vision of a better tomorrow might be more radical or more closely tied to your traditions.

For you, these stories can serve as a form of empowerment. I urge you to rewrite them to better align with your values or to write your own stories. Anyone can use the same tools I have used to create strategic narratives. You will need to base your version on the evidence of emerging trends and a basic understanding of the forces of change. You can start with the resources listed at the end of this book. Some will teach you how to research and think like a futurist. Others are excellent sources for gathering the latest information on the most critical trends, from technology and the environment to culture and politics.

Build on these resources to create your personal narratives. Share them with others. Use your visions for better tomorrows to recruit your own tribe of optimistic futurists. Empowered by these stories, you will create the rich tapestry that will become our better tomorrows.

Whichever path you choose, I hope this book has convinced you that we can reimagine our tomorrows. The most important skill to develop is a critical optimism about what is possible. After all, we humans are an incredible species. We emerged from caves to build villages, towns, cities, nations, and even explore the cosmos. As we come to the end of the industrial age, we should recognize how much we have accomplished in a short time. In less than 200 years, average life expectancy has doubled. In the last twenty years, the number of people living in extreme poverty has been cut in half. We are capable of making significant advances in relatively short time. Imagine what we might achieve in the next two decades.

I get it. We live in turbulent times. We face serious planet-wide challenges. It can seem naïve to be optimistic about tomorrow. But I believe that the very chaos we are experiencing represents the birth pains of a new world. We can use the tools of our digital age to empower individuals, conscious entrepreneurs, and communities, to create a future that is sustainable, equitable, and abundant.

If we choose, we can create a digital renaissance that will radically transform the way we live, work, and thrive. This future will be built from the bottom up. It will favor green technologies, social diversity, and economic fairness. It will bring with it a rebirth of optimism about the possibilities for all our tomorrows.

Our future begins with the stories we tell ourselves about what is possible. Your dreams have as much power as anyone else's in setting our course. Craft your stories using the tools of foresight, critical imagination, curiosity, and courage.

I can't wait to see what tomorrows you will imagine.

Resources

How To Think Like A Futurist

Hines, Andy & Peter Bishop, editors. *Thinking About the Future: Guidelines for Strategic Foresight.* Social Technologies, 2006.

Johansen, Bob. *Get There Early: Sensing the Future to Compete in the Present.* San Francisco: Berrett-Koehler Publishers, 2007.

King, Katie Bishop & Julia Rose West. *Futures Thinking Playbook.* CreateSpace, 2018.

Ogilvy, James A. *Creating Better Futures: Scenario Planning as a Tool for a Better Tomorrow.* New York: Oxford University Press, 2002.

Schwartz, Peter. *The Art of the Long View: Planning for the Future in an Uncertain World.* New York: Doubleday, 1991.

Slaughter, Richard, ed. *The Knowledge Base of Futures Studies: Professional Edition.* Foresight Int'l, 2005.

Wheelwright, Verne. *It's YOUR Future...Make It a Good One*! Harlingen: Personal Futures Network, 2010.

Visions Of Alternate Futures

Ashby, Madeline et. al. *Imagining the Future and Building It.* Intel, 2012.

Diamandis, Peter & Steven Kotler. *Abundance: The Future Is Faster Than You Think.* New York: Free Press, 2012.

Diamandis, Peter & Steven Kotler. *Bold: How to Go Big, Create Wealth and Impact the World.* New York: Simon & Schuster, 2016.

Frase, Peter. *Four Futures: Visions of the World After Capitalism.* Brooklyn: Verso, 2016.

Friedman, Thomas. *Thank You for Being Late: An Optimist's Guide to Thriving in the Age of Accelerations.* New York: Farrar, Straus and Giroux, 2016.

Ito, Joi & Jeff Howe. *Whiplash.* New York: Grand Central Publishing, 2016.

Jackson, Tim. *Prosperity Without Growth: Economics for a Finite Planet.* London: Earthscan, 2009.

Kelly, Kevin. *The Inevitable: Understanding 12 Technological Forces That Will Shape Our Future.* New York: Viking, 2016.

Khanna, Parag. *Connectography: Mapping the Future of Global Civilization.* New York: Random House, 2016.

Korten, David. *Change the Story, Change the Future: A Living Economy for a Living Earth.* Oakland: Berrett-Koehler Publishers, 2015.

Monbiot, George. *Out of the Wreckage: A New Politics for an Age of Crisis.* London: Verso, 2018.

Richard Florida. *The Rise of the Creative Class, Revisited.* Philadelphia: Basic Books, 2014.

Rivkin, Jeremy. *The Zero Marginal Cost Society.* New York: St. Martin's Press, 2015.

Suskind, Jamie. *Future Politics.* New York: Oxford University Press, 2018.

Online

This list represents the online sources I follow most closely. There are obviously many, many more resources online, including some great podcasts and video channels. I would highly recommend that you develop your own list and follow your favorite sources regularly.

Elevations: The Conscious Capitalism Blog. https://www.consciouscapitalism.org/blog

Forum for the Future. https://www.forumforthefuture.org/blogs

Futurism. https://futurism.com

Futurist Forum, Fast Company. https://www.fastcompany.com/section/futurist-forum

Institute for the Future. www.iftf.org

Net Impact. https://www.netimpact.org/blog

TED. https://www.ted.com

The Optimist Daily. https://www.optimistdaily.com

Triple Pundit: People, Planet, Profit. https://www.triplepundit.com

World Future Society. www.wfs.org

Yes! http://www.yesmagazine.org

Help Me Spread Optimsitic Futures

The decision to independently publish this book was an obvious one to me. How could I promote the idea of digital empowerment if I wasn't willing to embrace it for my own work? As I was researching and writing, I was also exploring the ways that the traditional publishing industry was being disrupted. What I have learned is that there is no better time to climb up on your personal soapbox and shout your ideas out to the world.

As powerful as these digital tools are we can only create better tomorrows if we amplify each other's voices. If you believe in these ideas, I need your help.

Share this book. Give it to a friend. Better yet buy copies for your colleagues and clients.

Go online and write a review. Share your thoughts on social media..#reimaginingtomorrows. Follow us on Facebook. https://www.facebook.com/ReimaginingOurTomorrows/

Become part of the OPTIMISTIC FUTURIST community.

Visit us at www.uniquevisions.net where you will find more resources to help you create your own stories of better tomorrows.

Join our Facebook group, Optimistic Futurists: Reimagining Our Tomorrows where you can share your stories with others who are also passionate about building a future that is sustainable, abundant and just.

And stay in touch.

joe@ uniquevisions.net

linkedin.com/in/joetankersley

@joe_tankersley

Acknowledgments

My work as a storyteller and futurist has been informed by ideas and insights generously shared by so many people over the years that I cannot begin to list them all. This is a meager attempt to acknowledge those most closely associated with the creation of the current work.

I have to start by thanking all of my colleagues in the professional futures community, the Association of Professional Futurists and the World Future Society, for sharing the tools and techniques they use to make sense of our possible futures. A special thanks to those fellow futurists who were instrumental in my early attempts to marry narrative and foresight; Emily Empel, Garry Golden, Lloyd Walker, Vanessa Timmer and the Disruptive Imaginings Collective. Scott Trowbridge and Trish Cerrone were great champions for this work inside Walt Disney Imagineering and generously carved out a space for us to play and experiment with new ways to imagine the future.

Suzanne Kingsbury is the person most responsible for the fact that this book actually got finished. As editor and writing coach she has been a patient taskmaster throughout; knowing exactly when I needed tough criticism or a positive nudge onward. Thanks also for the feedback provided by a group of steady readers; Amy Lynch, Jack Hoos, Jennifer Jarrett, Jenny Rhylee Hoang, Steve Seibert, Melissa Wade, Emily Empel and Marco Spilimbergo.

Libby Kingsbury's brilliant design sense and the critical eye of copy editor Heather Taylor are responsible for turning a mess of words into a book that is both beautiful and readable. Peggy Gilbart's meticulous proofreading gets credit for uncovering my penchant for comma abuse.

Just getting the words on the page is only a small part of sharing ideas in today's noisy marketplace. Succeeding in that herculean task would not be possible without the digital talents and social media expertise of April Koury, or the enthusiasm and professionalism of Sandra Smith and her team at Smith Publicity. Also, a big thanks to everyone who have recommended, endorsed and shared the book with friends and colleagues.

Finally, a special thanks goes to my wife, Susan Kroskey, for taking on the thankless task of living with a writer during the ups and downs of the creative process. Her unwavering support has given me the strength to remain optimistic about the possibility of creating better tomorrows.

About the Author

Joe Tankersley is a futurist, writer, and advocate for better tomorrows. He combines his experience as a storyteller with the tools of strategic foresight to help others create compelling visions for our futures.

His career has included stints as a filmmaker, screenwriter, educator, and Disney Imagineer. His entertainment and educational projects have been recognized nationally and internationally, and he is a recipient of the prestigious THEA award.

As part of Walt Disney Imagineering's elite Blue-Sky Studio, Joe helped establish the group's first Strategic Foresight Program and trained hundreds of Disney cast members to use his strategic narrative techniques. He led projects exploring the future of socially responsible corporations, creative communities, and digitally empowered workforces.

Since 2015, Joe has worked with nonprofits, entrepreneurs, community groups, and international corporations, intent on creating better tomorrows. Joe is passionate about projects that investigate the future of conscious capitalism, environmental sustainability, connected communities and digital empowerment.

Joe served on the board of directors for the Association of Professional Futurists for six years and was a founding board member of the Global Futures Forum. He currently serves as advisor to the Federal Alliance for Safe Homes and the UN Sustainable Tourism Observatory for Florida.

Joe lives in the heart of Central Florida, where if current trends continue, his future grandchildren will one day inherit beachfront property.